Published by
Princeton Architectural Press
37 East Seventh Street
New York, New York 10003

For a free catalog of books, call 1.800.722.6657.
Visit our website at www.papress.com.

Editor: Megan Carey
Designer: Jan Haux

Special thanks to: Bree Anne Apperley, Sara Bader, Nicola Bednarek
Brower, Janet Behning, Fannie Bushin, Carina Cha, Tom Cho, Penny (Yuen
Pik) Chu, Russell Fernandez, Linda Lee, John Myers, Katharine Myers,
Margaret Rogalski, Dan Simon, Andrew Stepanian, Jennifer Thompson,
Paul Wagner, Joseph Weston, and Deb Wood of Princeton Architectural
Press —Kevin C. Lippert, publisher

Front cover image:
James Casebere, *Green Staircase #1*, 2001. Digital chromogenic print.
60 x 48 inches and 96 x 77 inches. Copyright James Casebere. Courtesy
of James Casebere and Sean Kelly Gallery, New York

Back cover image, left:
Courtney Smith, *Bonito*, 2002. Cabinet and hand carving. Collection of
Elizabeth Moore, New York. Photograph by Rodrigo Pereda

Back cover image, right:
Petra Blaisse, Villa Leefdaal, Leefdaal, Belgium, 2003–4. Living room with
curtain pulled closed meeting the glass wall and landscape. Courtesy of
Inside Outside

Frontispiece image:
Planning study for space optimization in a vertically oriented, cylindrical
International Space Station module, 1997. Courtesy of Constance Adams

Library of Congress Cataloging-in-Publication Data
After taste : expanded practice in interior design / edited by Kent
Kleinman, Joanna Merwood-Salisbury, and Lois Weinthal. — 1st ed.
p. cm.
ISBN 978-1-61689-026-1 (alk. paper)
1. Interior decoration. I. Kleinman, Kent, 1956– II. Merwood-Salisbury,
Joanna. III. Weinthal, Lois. IV. Title: Expanded practice in interior design.
NK2125.A39 2011
747—dc22
                                    2011010530

After Taste

EXPANDED PRACTICE
IN INTERIOR DESIGN

Kent Kleinman,
Joanna Merwood-Salisbury,
and Lois Weinthal, editors

Princeton Architectural Press
New York

Contents

I

On the Problem of Taste

II

III

Introduction

Kent Kleinman, Joanna Merwood-Salisbury, and Lois Weinthal

Not only is th[e] accumulation of false richness unsavory, but above and before all, this taste for decorating everything around one is a false taste, an abominable little perversion.

—Le Corbusier

[Nineteenth-century] society gradually killed any creative impulse with the poison of its ruling taste.

—Sigfried Giedion

The repudiation of taste as a category by which to make and judge design is a defining trope of modern design criticism, and interior design is one of its primary targets. Starting in the eighteenth century the practice of designing interiors depended on the replication and display of highly coded aesthetic elements in order to signify intimate knowledge of the distinctions between social strata. For high modernist critics such as Le Corbusier and Sigfried Giedion, the techniques of this display were inherently suspicious, if not fundamentally flawed. Involving a surface application of decoration using the slippery feminine arts of disguise, interior design promoted architectural dishonesty and inauthenticity. For Giedion, the value of interior design was directly proportionate to its disappearance. In this rhetoric, interior design, viewed as a vehicle through which to communicate wealth and class affiliation, was a form of what economist Thorstein Veblen had labeled "conspicuous consumption," something that signified only to the degree that it resisted being actually useful, since uselessness was the measure of discretionary wealth. In this sense, interior design is close to fashion, and taste is code that enables both to serve their stratifying functions.

In fact, the historic links between interior design and taste are probably impossible to erase: the creation and design of private space is essential to the construction of the modern social world and its manners. Indeed, one could say that the very purpose of interior design has been to "demonstrate the prevailing taste."[1] The inextricable interconnectedness of the two, along with the persistent gendering of interior design as feminine, has shaped both the vocational and intellectual development of the field. It has created a form of practice with highly specialized techniques, methods, and knowledge domains, a practice situated outside of architecture and outside of fine art but tangential to both. Intellectually, however, this partitioning has made it difficult for historians and critics of interior design to establish a theoretical framework for the field. Only recently, but rapidly multiplying, has there been critical and scholarly writing on interior design.

Despite the importance of taste to the formation and constitution of the discipline, it has not been subject to examination, with a few notable exceptions.[2] The essays in this volume interrogate the idea of taste, its importance to the history and practice of interior design (including emphatic attempts to reject it in the mid-twentieth century), before positing its continued usefulness in the field today, albeit in renewed terms. Our intent is to resist the temptation to examine the history and theory of the discipline through the lens of other fields (especially architecture, through which it will always be seen as inferior) and to leverage the philosophical concept central to interior design's own tradition.

Early versions of the essays collected here were presented at *After Taste*, an annual symposium series hosted by Parsons The New School of Design between 2007 and 2010. Created to provide an intellectual framework for a graduate program in interior design, this series was dedicated to the critical study of the interior, offering expansive views of interior studies, highlighting emerging areas of research, identifying allied practices, making public its under-explored territory, and attracting future designers and scholars to the field. When first conceived, the title was deliberately chosen to signal a move away from the popular image of interior design as a field of taste making and tastemakers. In the course of its short life, the *After Taste* project has continued to evolve. The purpose of this book is not to publish the proceedings of the symposium series but to edit, refine, and even challenge the premise of that forum. To our surprise, taste has emerged as an important and continually relevant intellectual framework. As one of these essays proposes, perhaps a better title is not *After Taste*, but *After After Taste*, or *Taste, After All*.

The book is organized into three sections. The first, "On the Problem of Taste," investigates the historical connectedness between the discipline of interior design and the philosophical concept of taste. Beginning in the eighteenth century, the modern interior was established in parallel with the invention of the modern subject, a subject who occupies a separate and private realm apart from his or her public persona, both spatially and psychologically. The second, "Expanded Pedagogies and Methods," maps the twentieth-century territory of interior design practice and pedagogy. The section pays special attention to attempts to redefine and expand the field of its operation beginning in the 1960s, attempts that embrace the social sciences and environmental psychology as well as new technologies of construction and representation, often in the service of inter- or transdisciplinarity. The final section, "Practicing After Taste," gathers these diverse threads together focusing on some particular concerns within contemporary practice: accommodating shifting definitions of what is properly "public" and "private"; the problem of recognizing, recording, and preserving the ephemeral quality of interiors; and finally the terrestrial insights to be gained through the design of extraterrestrial interiors.

Within these sections the contributions take three basic forms: essays by historians and critics, interviews with practitioners on the margins of normative practice, and portfolios featuring the work of contemporary artists and designers. This structure spans a range of contemporary efforts aimed at recuperating some of the discipline-specific attributes of interior design, which, paradoxically, have oftentimes migrated into adjacent domains, such as the fine arts. It provides a platform for a good deal of thematic cross-referencing of diverse genres of practice. For example Courtney Smith's de- and reconstructions of period furniture pieces echo the same concern with personal identity (especially femininity) and decoration described in essays by Penny Sparke and Anthony Vidler. James Casebere's photographs and the cinematic decors of Stephen and Timothy Quay explore the same narrative possibilities of the interior and its representation that Julieanna Preston identifies as essential to interior design if it is to maintain its historical concern with perceptual awareness, subjectivity, and interpretation. Finally the diverse and innovative practices of Petra Blaisse and Inside Outside investigate a body-centric tactility that surprisingly proves central to housing bodies in outer space, as Constance Adams's work at NASA demonstrates.

This collection is intended to spur further scholarship and work in the field of interior design. Many significant topics are only touched upon here, and others are not treated at all. The history of taste remains, we believe, a profound intellectual touchstone for theorizing interior studies, and the eighteenth century is the temporal nexus of this discourse. The twenty-first century, however, demands that the interior be framed in performative terms. Rapid urbanization will accelerate the need for a theory of adaptive reuse and preservation, and emerging technologies are changing basic spatial taxonomies. In short, we hope with this collection to entice others to do more in a field well worth the study.

The epigraphs to the introduction are from Le Corbusier, *The Decorative Art of Today*, trans. James Dunnett (1925; Cambridge, MA: MIT Press, 1987), 90; and Sigfried Giedion, *Space, Time and Architecture: The Growth of a New Tradition* (1941; Cambridge, MA: Harvard University Press, 1982), 277.

1   Robin Evans, "The Developed Surface: An Enquiry into the Brief Life of an Eighteenth-Century Drawing Technique," *9H*, no. 8 (1989), 121.

2   Penny Sparke, *As Long as It's Pink: The Sexual Politics of Taste* (London: Pandora, 1995).

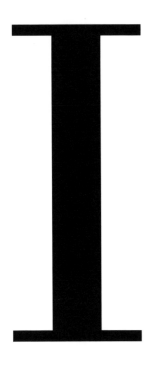

On the Problem of Taste

TASTE AND THE INTERIOR DESIGNER

Penny Sparke

The concept of taste is central to the historical and contemporary definition of interior design and of the interior designer. Historically, interior design has been identified with feminine taste, and this has led to its marginalization, especially by architects.[1] The gap that grew up, through the late nineteenth century and early twentieth century, between the fashion- and style-oriented modern interior and an alternative model developed by the modernist architect, one that set out to eradicate the very existence of an interior that could be distinguished from the architectural shell, has grown almost unbridgeable. A study of the modern interior through the lens of taste allows us to focus on the experience and the aesthetic of what has been called "feminine modernity."[2]

The word "taste" is sometimes used on its own, as an absolute concept, and sometimes joined by the epithets "good" or "bad." The reasons for this are historically rooted. In the preindustrial context, when it was only the aristocracy that had the wherewithal to engage in the possession and display of artworks and luxury items in their interior settings, there was no need to add a qualifier to the term. In that context taste was a universally recognized, absolute value without a polarized set of meanings contained within it. In his little book, *Bricobracomania: The Bourgeois and the Bibelot,* Remy G. Saisselin addressed this issue and explained that the nobility was expected to possess art as it defined, and was inseparable from, their rank and social function.[3] The possession of art was, he explained, synonymous at that time with the ideas of landed wealth and lineage. He also suggested that it was ownership by the nobility that conferred status upon artworks, not the other way round.

With the arrival of industrialization, and the extension to the middle classes of the ownership of art—of, that is, the possibility of large swathes of society possessing taste—that formula reversed itself, however, and the artwork, often expressed in interior décor itself, acquired the capacity to confer status on its owners. Redolent with associations from an earlier, more socially stable era, it brought those meanings into a new age characterized by social mobility. As a result, Saisselin elaborated, the work of art, in that new context, was defined first and foremost by its marketability and was transformed, as a consequence, into what he called a "bibelot," the decorative content of domestic interiors. Indeed it was in the interior that the bibelot acquired its meaning. Through its presence in that location the social status and identity of its owners were formed, expressed, and put on display. In short, taste could be bought in the marketplace and brought home.

Alongside that important shift of meaning for the artwork or luxury possession, the possibility of its mass production through the advancement of technology introduced the existence of both unique, or authentic, art objects and of factory-made bibelots that acted as substitutes for them. In turn this created a climate in which a body of design reformers, led by A. W. N. Pugin, John Ruskin, and William Morris, surfaced whose sole aim was to defend authenticity and to condemn its opposite. In the process, the polarized concepts of good and bad taste came into being and were discussed in numerous texts, including Pugin's text *Contrasts*, and addressed by exhibitions such as Henry Cole's *Chamber of Horrors*.[4] The assumption was that the new middle-class consumer needed to be educated about taste. A dichotomy also emerged between a realistic, pragmatic idea of the interior that was linked with middle-class values and aspirations, and a more idealistic version of it that was seen, primarily, as a location for the reform of aesthetic and moral values.[5] The latter brought with it a focus on the meaning and design of the domestic interior and the artifacts within it.

In spite of the fact that the Victorian design reformers focused on individual objects (furniture and the decorative arts in particular) and the later modernists presented their discussions and proposals in the context of architecture, the interior—defined either by its material components or, spatially, through its links with its architectural shell—became the site where the fiercest battles about taste were fought. These same battles came to a head in the twentieth century in the growing tension between the interior decorator and the interior designer.

The aestheticization of the middle-class interior, its links with feminine culture and modernity, and its role as an expression of newly acquired social status and identity were fully in place by the end of the nineteenth century. By the early twentieth century the interior decorator had emerged as the main agent whose task it was to ensure the existence and continuation of those complex socio-cultural relationships. That new profession's role was to inject good taste into interiors whose inhabitants lacked the capacity or confidence to do it themselves. The emergence of a new professional role for women was an important component of this development. In the United Kingdom, for example, cousins Rhoda and Agnes Garrett were among the first women to make a living for themselves by decorating other peoples' homes, while in the United States women such as Candace Wheeler and a handful of others moved

into the same arena. The career of the pioneer American interior decorator, Elsie de Wolfe, is particularly interesting in this context. It was de Wolfe who fully developed the potential of the role of the interior decorator as tastemaker. **Fig. 1** Having risen through the ranks of society from a fairly humble middle-class background (her father was a doctor and she was brought up in a New York brownstone which she had found ugly), and cognizant of the important relationship between social aspiration and its material accoutrements, she was well prepared for that role. Also, through her first career as an actress on the Broadway stage, she had learned firsthand about the workings of the relationship between the stage set and the characters played out on it, and she was quick to transfer that knowledge to the domestic interior. In addition, in that her first interior project was undertaken in her own home on Irving Place in New York, she crossed the divide between the world of amateur feminine domesticity and that of professional interior decoration, blurring the boundaries between them. **Figs. 2, 3** As a result she rapidly acquired a deep understanding of the ways in which

Fig. 1
**Elsie de Wolfe in the drawing
room of her home, 122 East
Seventeenth Street, New
York City**
Frontispiece to Elsie de Wolfe,
The House in Good Taste, 1913

the decoration of the interior can, through the application of taste, play a role in status and identity formation and dissemination, and the importance of women's engagement with modernity in that process.

De Wolfe's preferred decorating style was eighteenth-century French, both Louis XV and XVI. In developing an interior aesthetic that would suggest an elevated social status for her clients, she looked to an era in which the notions of aristocracy, material luxury, and taste had been inextricably intertwined and were understood unproblematically. In early twentieth-century America, in the context of her second-generation nouveau riche clientele, the meanings of those styles remained unambiguous. Many of de Wolfe's clients were the sons and daughters of industrialists and businessmen who had made their money in the boom years of the late nineteenth

Fig. 2
Elsie de Wolfe's dining room,
before redecoration, 1896
From Elsie de Wolfe, *The House*
in Good Taste, 1913

century. However, although the styles she used recalled an era in which the concept of taste had been defined in absolute terms, de Wolfe's famous advice book of 1913 was titled *The House in Good Taste*, rather than, as would have been more likely in the eighteenth century, *The House in Taste*.[6] She was working at a time when a singular sense of taste no longer existed; the result of the design reformers who had rallied against what they saw as the betrayal of taste and who now understood taste in terms of the polar opposites, "good" and "bad" taste. The word "good" was a necessary inclusion for de Wolfe, therefore, and she spelled out its advantages to her potential clients, against what was still considered by many to be the bad taste of the alternative, i.e., the dark and cluttered spaces of the Victorian middle-class interior. In spite of their explicit historicism, through their lightness and their brightness, de Wolfe presented

Fig. 3
Elsie de Wolfe's dining room,
after redecoration, 1898
From Elsie de Wolfe, *The House*
in Good Taste, 1913

her interiors as modern, tasteful substitutes to those that had preceded them. In one sense, they had features in common with other progressive interiors of that era, including those of the arts and crafts movement in the United Kingdom (created by M. H. Baillie Scott and C. R. Mackintosh); the proto-modernist interiors of the members of the Viennese Werkstätte; and the United States' own pioneering modernist, Frank Lloyd Wright. Where de Wolfe's spaces differed from those contemporary interiors, however, was in their overt reference to taste and social class, in her lack of interest in their architectural shells (they were theater sets in that sense), and in their strong interaction with the identities of their (usually female) inhabitants.

De Wolfe was perhaps even more modern than many of her proto-modern contemporaries in her understanding of the role of taste, or rather of good taste, and the part it played in her clients' decisions to employ an interior decorator. Through her inclusion of art objects in her interiors, and her links with what in a masculine context was called "collecting" but which was called "shopping" in the context of feminine culture, she had an intimate appreciation of the workings of taste. While her work was mostly with, and for, women—either themselves as clients or as the wives of clients—for whom she created both private and public spaces, the handful of projects she undertook for men, among them Henry Clay Frick and Condé Nast, demonstrated her deep understanding of the role of the interior decorator in creating spaces within which the concept of taste was their preeminent feature. **Fig. 4**

While de Wolfe was content to work with the notion of the unified, self-contained, architecture-free interior, and she saw no problem in offering her "good taste" to clients who were less sure about their own and therefore happy to pay someone else to inject their taste into their living spaces, the European and American progressive architects and designers of the early decades of the twentieth century approached the interior rather differently. For them it was not a question of either good or bad taste but rather of no taste at all. Those architects associated the concept of taste with feminine modernity, bourgeois domesticity, fashion, decoration, and conspicuous consumption. In search of a means of sidestepping those areas, they developed a modern architectural formula that looked to rational, contemporary developments in science and technology instead of the "irrational" world of feminine modernity. From the *Gesamtkunstwerke* of the art nouveau and *Jugendstil* architects through to the functionalism of the Bauhaus,

Fig. 4
Condé Nast's apartment, 1040
Park Avenue, New York City,
ca. 1925

Fig. 5
View out from interior,
Le Corbusier, Villa Savoye,
Poissy, France, 1928–31

Le Corbusier, and others, the modernist architects and designers defined the interior as an extension of the architectural shell and they proposed a new definition of it that all but denied its very existence. **Fig. 5**

From the 1860s onwards, many of the anxieties of the design reformers, and subsequently those of the modernists, focused on what they saw as a worrying relationship of commerce with design and the attendant forces of trade and retail. Linked to both class and gender (but primarily to the latter), their primary fear was that a reversal of the relationship between art and social status that Saisselin had outlined would mean the end to the idea of taste as an absolute value and the emergence of a relativism that would seriously undermine it. They saw that threat located in the domestic interior and, more specifically, in the hands of the housewife-decorator and the (often female) professional interior decorator. Seeking to rebuild a world of absolute values, the modernists turned away from the commercial arena and the context of pragmatism to the seemingly safe, quantitative measures of science and technology. In creating inside spaces, therefore, they looked to the public sphere, production-oriented, process-focused new spaces of the factory and office that had been created with the help of scientific management engineers and space planners. From the work of Christine Frederick in the United States through that of Ernst May, working with Grete Schütte-Lihotsky in Frankfurt in the 1920s, the systematic approach of step-saving, of, that is, finding the quickest and most efficient means of performing work—a methodology that was first undertaken on factory floors—was applied to domestic kitchens. **Fig. 6**

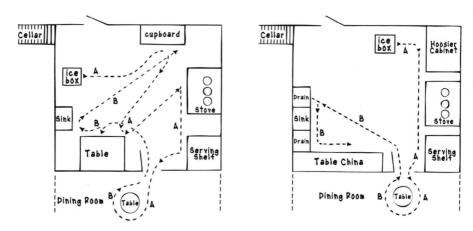

Fig. 6
Floor plans of a poorly
arranged kitchen and a
well-arranged kitchen
demonstrate how to create
an efficient workflow.
Originally published in Christine
Frederick, *You and Your Kitchen*,
1914

The result was a new kind of domestic space planning that had function, rather than social status, at its core. The new approach went beyond the kitchen. In his little house for Truus Schröder-Schrader, for example, the Dutch architect-designer Gerrit Rietveld developed an interior that was characterized by flexibility and functionality following the principles of a traditional Japanese house. This was interior design that operated outside the requirements of taste. Rather, what was at stake was the creation of an effective machine for living in, encouraging a life that valued simplicity, classlessness, and social engagement over social status.

The modernist domestic interior developed through the 1920s continuing to borrow from the public sphere in order to minimize the relationship of the home with trade, consumption, bourgeois domesticity, and, most importantly, the concept of taste. Le Corbusier not only formed ideas about transparency, indoor/outdoor ambiguity, and the use of industrial materials and fitted furniture in the home—all of which became aesthetic prerequisites of the modern dwelling—as means of emphasizing his rejection of bourgeois domesticity, he also borrowed freestanding furniture pieces from outside the home, among them the chaise longue and the leather club armchair. **Fig. 7** He found the first in the tuberculosis sanatorium and the latter in the gentleman's club, both areas which stood outside the remit of taste and served to reinforce the focus on functionality and public masculinity in the modernist home. Interestingly, the reference to the gentleman's club did not completely write domestic comfort out of the picture but reflected, rather, an alternative model of domesticity that, rather than being rooted within feminine culture, was built on the idea of masculine conviviality.

The idea, or ideal, of not bad taste but rather of non-taste that defined the modernist domestic interior also underpinned the vision of the interior designer who, born in the early post–Second World War years, took his (mostly men) lead from architectural modernism and worked predominantly in the public sphere. The interior decorator (mostly women)/interior designer (mostly men) battle began in earnest in the 1940s and it has continued to wage since then. Although the two terms were often used interchangeably to some extent, there was a strong sense that while the decorators shopped and arranged things that already existed, and had little interest in the architectural shell, the designers worked holistically, emphasized the interior's dependence on the architecture, and designed items *ex novo*. By that time the industrial designer had

Fig. 7 (top)
Chaise longue, designed by
Le Corbusier with Pierre
Jeanneret and Charlotte
Perriand, 1928

Fig. 8 (bottom)
Overstuffed Victorian parlor
is an example of bad taste, in
Odd Brockmann, *Good and
Bad Taste*, 1955

also become a force to be reckoned with. He (usually men) was also seen as an innovator—one whose main allegiance was to the manufacturing industry—rather than as someone who simply supplied what clients wanted. The decorators were condemned for their closeness to their clients, their traditionalism, their links with trade (several had shops), and, above all, for their continued commitment to good taste as a means of expressing social status and identity.

By the post–Second World War years, however, the high-minded idealism that had reinforced architectural modernism had, in turn, engendered another fashionable, market-led style, often dubbed "contemporary." A 1955 text, titled *Good or Bad Taste*, written by Norwegian Odd Brockmann, showed that very little had changed since the nineteenth century inasmuch as the threat to good taste was still the overstuffed Victorian parlor. **Fig. 8** The humanized modern interior, which proposed an antidote to bad taste, had, by 1955, become synonymous with good taste. Within the contemporary interior art, as a marker of taste, was no longer a bibelot—it had become absorbed into the interior design. As Brockmann explained, "We must admit that our interiors have gained a lot in sense of harmonious restfulness, spaciousness and order."[7] These aesthetic values did not need the confirmation of a painting on the wall or a statuette on the sideboard. Arguably the interior itself had become the bibelot, the marker of good taste and of social distinction.

The definition of taste as a socio-cultural construct, promoted by Pierre Bourdieu in his book *Distinction: A Social Critique of the Judgement of Taste*, meant that the phenomenon could not be understood as an absolute but rather as being socially and culturally determined.[8] The level of education underpinning a taste decision in, say, the purchase of a sofa, or a meal, or a piece of recorded music, Bourdieu explains, determines the level of the sophistication of, or knowledge about, its art content. This helps to explain the continued popularity of the minimal interior, the architectural and design equivalent of nouveau cuisine, which represents the stylistic legacy of ideological modernism and the shift from its alignment with "no taste" to its becoming a marker of "good taste." Put simply, the discussion about good and bad design, an updated, post-1945 version of the nineteenth-century design reformers' good/bad taste debate, coincided with the transformation of modernism into a marketable style and arguably signified a softening of the boundary between the decorator and the designer.

There is just one more point I would like to make in my romp through the history of twentieth-century taste, in which I have discussed the concept as an absolute, aristocratic value; the binary system of good and bad taste; the modernists' commitment to non-taste; and the completion of a full circle with the impossibility of any escape, in the context of late capitalism and the power of the marketplace, from the good taste/bad taste binary system. In the early twenty-first century, we inhabit a postmodern world in which taste has become a relative concept: increased globalization and multiculturalism have produced a proliferation of discrete taste cultures that may not share a common language and are judged to be either good or bad dependent upon the perspective from which they are being viewed. In that complex landscape of diverse taste values, the countless popular television programs that focus on revamping interiors come into their own and we return to the idea of the interior as a theater set with which de Wolfe was so comfortable. If we take Bourdieu's idea of taste as a socio-cultural construct to its logical conclusion, and we combine it with the highly mediatized, postmodern idea of fragmented and multiple identities, and of multiple movements through society, rather than the existence of a fixed, linear social hierarchy, then, I would suggest, we have to accept the idea of the coexistence of multiple tastes and the interior decorator/designer's responsibility to design for them. This may make people trained within the modernist ethos deeply uncomfortable, but whether we like it or not, those popular television programs seem to be doing something right.

1   Penny Sparke, *As Long as It's Pink: The Sexual Politics of Taste* (London: Pandora, 1995).

2   Alison Light, *Forever England: Femininity, Literature and Conservatism between the Wars* (London: Routledge, 1991).

3   Remy G. Saisselin, *Bricobracomania: The Bourgeois and the Bibelot* (London: Thames and Hudson, 1985).

4   A. W. N. Pugin, *Contrasts: Or, A Parallel between the Noble Edifices of the Middle Ages, and Corresponding Buildings of the Present Day Showing the Present Decay of Taste* (London, 1841). Henry Cole's so-called *Chamber of Horrors* exhibition was held in Marlborough House in London in 1852.

5   Charles Rice, *The Emergence of the Interior: Architecture, Modernity, Domesticity* (London: Routledge, 2007).

6   Elsie de Wolfe, *The House in Good Taste* (New York: The Century Co., 1913).

7   Odd Brockmann, *Good or Bad Taste* (1955; Littlehampton, UK: Littlehampton Book Service, 1970), 22.

8   Pierre Bourdieu, *Distinction: A Social Critique of the Judgement of Taste* (1979; repr., Cambridge, MA: Harvard University Press: 1984; London: Routledge & Kegan Paul, 1986).

TASTE, AFTER ALL

Kent Kleinman

Oh, those Greeks! They knew how to live. What is required for that is to stop courageously at the surface, the fold, the skin, to adore appearance, to believe in forms, tones, words, in the whole Olympus of appearance. Those Greeks were superficial—out of profundity. And is this not precisely what we are coming back to…?

—Friedrich Nietzsche

SUPERFICIAL/TASTE

I want to make a case for the importance of interior design based on its origins in what has historically been argued as its unique weaknesses. The plural form is intentional, for there are not one but two attributes of interior design that have traditionally dogged the field and served to negatively differentiate it, in an almost reflexive fashion, from architecture (e.g., architecture is what interiors is not). I am referring to the field's preoccupation with the surface of things at the expense of depth, and its reliance on, indeed identity with, matters of taste. In criticisms of interior design, shallowness and taste are at times conflated into one composite vulnerability: matters of taste, as particularized and subjective experiences, can never be coercively argued (*individuum est ineffabile*) and thus can never achieve the solidity and firmness of matters of fact, and matters of fact, we are told, do not reside on the mere surface of things. But my goal is to build a strong case for interiors, so I will attempt to argue for both the status of the surface and the status of judgments of taste as independently important endeavors. I hope, of course, that interior studies will not, in an attempt to dodge its critics, choose to divorce itself from its long partnership with taste making and superficiality, will not, in other words, retreat into "interior architecture."

ON THE SURFACE

Language establishes a strong connection between knowing and digging. How does one access knowledge: by burrowing beneath the surface of appearances and plumbing the depths to uncover, reveal, unearth, mine, excavate, extract, and dredge out nuggets of wisdom up from the bedrock of certainty into the contingent light of day. Knowledge has a locus and it is never on the surface, always in depth. Virtue is deep; knowledge is most reliable when deep; earnestness is substantiated by depth; authenticity is validated depth; we drink deeply at wells of wisdom and still surfaces run deep if they aren't just puddles. The deep is signifier for the true. This equation sets in motion a relationship that is equally effective when the polarities are reversed. If depth is the locus of value and its sign is positive, then shallowness is the locus of valuelessness and its sign is negative. This is why book covers purportedly lead to poor judgments, why an inauthentic person is shallow, why a lazy person just scratches the surface, and why you are asked to occasionally look deep into your soul and not stare at your navel.

This model informs Western theories of knowledge. By stripping away layers to find deep essences we also strip away the particular, the idiosyncratic, the "merely surface" material in search of the general, the universal, or at least the most widely applicable. Particularization is a habit of the simple mind. The most vivid example of this tendency is also one of the earliest: Plato modeled the entire sensible world as ontologically transient, unreliable, and deceptive, a mere instance of immutable forms residing elsewhere. For Plato the entire sensible world was shallow.

The counter notion, namely that depth is not the only place to look for knowledge, is of somewhat recent vintage but widely embraced by those with a semiological bent. One of the most adamant critics of the methodological shovel, and one of the most lucid advocates of a mode of inquiry that does not involve digging, was the anthropologist Clifford Geertz. In 1973, Geertz published an essay titled "Thick Description: Towards an Interpretive Theory of Culture," the opening chapter in the influential volume *The Interpretation of Cultures*.[1] Geertz's project was to demonstrate that cultural anthropology is not like science with its attendant laws, but like literature with its attendant interpretations. Laws reside under particulars, but interpretations reside on top of them. The first are excavated; the second are constructed. If you want to learn something of what it means to be human, writes Geertz, you need to "read" not universal human subjects—since they do not exist—but particular subjects acting out specific cultural scenes within a net of particular codes. Only highly concrete and specific, what Geertz calls "thick," descriptions can capture the cultural logic of a given human moment. Thick description is a term borrowed from the British philosopher Gilbert Ryle.[2] It begins with painstakingly close attention to the particular surface conditions of an event or setting and involves a microscopic sweep of the relevant eventscape, a detective-like scrutiny for hints and clues. In fact, the detective novel is often cited as the paradigm for this form of knowledge production.

If one wishes to counter the considerable weight of the science of depth, which is in fact nothing less than the positive science of lawful, abstract truths and demonstrable falsehoods, the science that Karl Popper lauded as "one of the greatest spiritual adventures that man has yet known," one has to posit some kind of alternate model of knowing the world.[3] And for such a model, one cannot do better than to turn to a remarkable essay by the Italian historian Carlo Ginzburg titled "Morelli, Freud and

Sherlock Holmes: Clues and Scientific Method."[4] Although Ginzburg's article bears no direct relationship to interior design, its ambition is to sketch out a science of the hint or the clue as the source of knowledge, a science that runs parallel to positive science, one "learnt not from books but from listening, from doing, from watching... [that] could not make use of the powerful and terrible tool of abstraction."[5] Precisely such a science is useful to recover for interior studies, for it constitutes a history that legitimizes specificity and particularity as knowledge domains.

In "Morelli, Freud and Sherlock Holmes," Ginzburg describes a series of articles by one Giovanni Morelli, an Italian physician and art collector, who, writing under the pseudonym of a Russian art historian in the mid-1870s, introduced a novel method for the correct attribution of old master paintings. The method was based not on discerning grand compositional motives or recognizing elusive evocative qualities or underlying structural attributes. Rather, it rested on discovering the unintended yet highly individualistic rendering of minutia—the shape of an ear, the articulation of a hand, the configuration of a fingernail, and other such details. Morelli's method was based on clues unwittingly left by the artist, like a fingerprint that reveals correct identity, or idiosyncratic flourishes neglected by a forger that could unmask an imposter. Ginzburg notes the remarkable similarity between Morelli's transformation of the art gallery into a lineup of clues ("any art gallery studied by Morelli begins to resemble a rogues' gallery"[6]) and the "morellizing" methods of Sherlock Holmes, right down to the detective's ability to identify the provenance of a pair of severed ears, a feat displayed in the strange case titled "The Cardboard Box." The capacity for such minor clues to reveal identity is, of course, resonant with Freud's elevation of the offhanded detail or behavioral gaffe as exposing important truths, and indeed Freud was impressed with and influenced by Morelli's method:

> It seems to me that [Morelli's] method of inquiry is closely related to the technique of psychoanalysis. It, too, is accustomed to divine secret and concealed things from despised or unnoticed features, from the rubbish-heap, as it were, of our observations.[7]

Not coincidently, the "rubbish-heap...of our observations" is also where Geertz spent a good deal of his time and intellectual energy, for the richly textured detail that anchors his interpretations of local cultures was not to be found in gross generalizations or abstract structures, but rather in the particulars of observed action, in the thickness of his descriptive field notes.

Morelli's method participates in a larger epistemological trajectory rooted in symptomology that encompasses medical semiotics (the physician's use of revealing signs that point to an unseen disease); psychoanalysis (the analyst's attention to marginal details and unintentional slips of the tongue); and criminology (the systematic and accurate identification of individuals via fingerprints for the maintenance of judicial order and via graphology for the administration of contract law). Ginzburg identifies this as a semiotic approach to knowing, a model of knowledge based on the interpretation of clues. Morelli's, Freud's, and Holmes's rescued observations are the deviant decorative flourishes and idiosyncratic details that are eliminated in any science based on norms, statistical averages, and the typical. Instead, they constitute a science of the individualized event, the particularized act.

In resurrecting the Morellian method, Ginzburg is clearly after a prize much more significant than a reliable method of connoisseurship. He is reconstructing the lineage of a type of knowledge based on the wisdom that unites communities without the virtue of "terminological precision."[8] It is knowledge based on experience, such as looking at the gait of a horse and judging its health, or the artisanal knowledge represented by the silent rubbing together of fingers with eyes closed to test a material, or the intuitive confidence associated with great intimacy, a conjectural mode of knowing. It is knowledge that "might not even be reducible to words," that goes under the name "folklore" or "fable." This form of knowing progressively disappears from the folios of formal treatises in the Enlightenment, and emerges instead in the pages of the late eighteenth- and early nineteenth-century novels of the bourgeoisie.[9]

This final observation offers a useful link back to our subject, for the novel is interior's sibling art form. The highly descriptive, intimate, and detailed narration that is an essential, if often belittled, part of the legacy of interior design thinking and writing is undoubtedly modeled on the novelistic voice. This voice avoids statements of principle or sweeping declarations; it shuns grand compositional structures and favors instead the descriptive mode and the internal dialogue. It focuses on particulars, on the circumstantial, on clues and indexes that stand outside of the general sweep of historical narrative. It stands in contrast to the positivistic claims of enlightenment science, and is instead the source of critical "little insights" and, in the genre of the *Bildungsroman*, offers education in essential societal initiation rights. The novelistic voice is assembled of details that knowing subjects decode to reveal secrets of identity and motive, as in this minor but typical sample:

> ...a visit by Princess Margaret and Lord Snowden [sic] to Greentree... prompted the freshening of the entire guest wing, including, for the royal visitors, two bedrooms, a sitting room, and bath....To remind the Queen's sister that she was in America, the new bed with a cotton matelasse headboard was given a graphic patchwork quilt, and the floor was scattered with a number of small hooked rugs.[10]

This is not Gustave Flaubert, but rather Albert Hadley. This is a form of descriptive narration that is able, as architectural writing rarely can, to reflect an interior state and social narrative by intricate attention to telling details. Flaubert of course regularly used just such descriptions of the interior:

> ...she spent the first few days planning changes in the house. She took the shades off the candlesticks, had new wallpaper hung, the stairs repainted, and benches placed round the sundial in the garden; she even made enquiries about installing a fish pond, with its own fountain.[11]

The history I am sketching here is that of the suppressed science of lore, divination, reading of clues, and embodied experience that is the wellspring of the design disposition that characterizes interior design. It is an affair with the surface, based on life in its specificity and particularity, based on attention to details that have currency in social commerce, a knowledge capable of inductive judgments founded on the reading of subtle hints and predictive judgments based on a joint communal body of experience. This model of knowledge, traced by Ginzburg, named by Ryle ("thick description"), and operationalized by Geertz, offers a framework for taking seriously the surface details of things. If you strip away the details and try to get behind or beneath the surface you are moving in precisely the wrong epistemological direction since the surface provides the fixed points, the revealing clues, for layer upon layer of interpretative strata. The result of thick description is a rich, stratified, wobbly pile of increasingly nuanced readings anchored on the surface of the phenomenal world.

A direct spinoff of this paradigm is the explosion of aesthetic practices and scholarship that treat the most individualized of surfaces, namely skin, as a site for creative and cultural expression. The notion of treating skin as a site of signification is certainly not new. Nudity as a form of costume was an exalted and particular feature of classical Greek society, in which nudity was attire reserved for select athletic youths only, whereas nakedness was otherwise generally banned.[12] The skin was, so to speak, a stratum on which was inscribed a widely legible social code. In the agora, it was entirely possible to be inappropriately naked, or properly nude. But if skin as a site for cultural signification is not new, scholarship on it is. Clothing, not skin, has long held the status as the signifying layer of the body. But the boundary between culture and nature, clothing and skin, has now become problematized to the point where the skin itself is considered not a boundary at all—i.e., not a site of demarcation—but a marginal zone—i.e., a site where distinctions are blurred and leaks between self and society occur.[13] There are many examples to cite of artistic practices that are sited on the skin itself, from Jenny Holzer's work *Lustmord*, with quotes from victims of war, rape, and murder inscribed on detail-rich fields of flesh rather than traditional neutral "ground," to Stelarc's body suspensions of the late 1970s and early 1980s, to Orlan's staged multiple cosmetic surgeries. But possibly the most groundbreaking work in this genre was only partially an aesthetic project and principally a medical one, namely the famous 1995 Vacanti Mouse, an immune-depressed mouse with a ear grown on its back for eventual transplantation to ear-trauma victims. With this event the skin as medical site became conflated with its cultural and aesthetic associations.

A final observation on the surface as the stratum for a science for interior studies concerns the female-gendered character of both the field of practice and the field of knowledge. This similarity is no coincidence. To note that interior design is historically a feminized craft rooted in domesticity and homemaking is obvious. Less obvious is the feminization of skin and shallowness and the binary masculinization of structure and depth. In her cultural study of skin, Claudia Benthien notes that there are really two culturally defined skins—a male version which registers the rippling anatomical features lying beneath the surface and that, if removed, reveals knowledge of the bodily structure; and the female version that is smooth and opaque and that is almost never removed unless to disclose the nested voids of the reproductive organs.[14] **Figs. 1, 2** There are virtually no female *écorchés*. The male body is the anatomical norm, and renderings of flayed bodies and delayered anatomical studies are modeled overwhelmingly on the male figure. As Benthien notes, "the coding of femaleness takes place on the skin, that of maleness under the skin—that is how we could characterize the juxtaposition that...remains valid for many centuries."[15] In visualizing the anatomy of a building, the didactic exposure of the structure and various support systems of architecture made possible by graphically removing the building skin is analogous to a kind of flaying. The exploded axonometric is not that different from Vesalius's *écorchés*; one might even say there is an epistemological continuity between the two forms of *representing* the location of knowledge which has allowed architecture to depict itself in relation to the birth of modern science. The issue of representation in interior design, as in anatomy, is fascinating territory if one challenges the (male gendered) norm and accepts the (female gendered) significance of surface particularity. The all too familiar material swatches comprising scraps of coordinated finish samples, or even the tradition of highly articulated interior perspectives are, of course, an inadequate response to this challenge. The decors of the Quay brothers, or the photographic milieus of James Casebere, offer more provocative alternatives to the default norm of architectural abstraction.

TASTE

Taste is a concept that clings to interior design and has served both to establish its value and bracket it off from architecture proper. The term appears with the frequency of a well-orchestrated branding exercise: from Elsie de Wolfe's seminal 1913 book *The House in Good Taste* to the opening chapter of Billy Baldwin's 1972 monograph *Taste and Logic in Decorating* to the nom de plume of the former *Home & Garden* editor Mayer Rus, aka *The Testy Tastemaker*. Contemporary and high modern critical discourse only

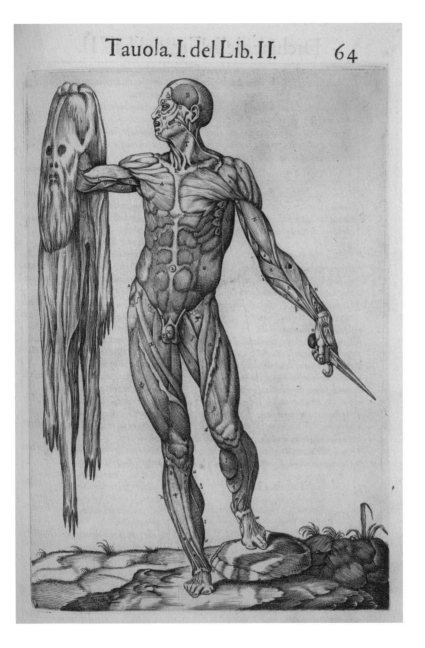

Fig. 1
Male figure, from Juan
de Valverde de Hamusco,
*Historia de la composicion
del cuerpo humano*, 1556

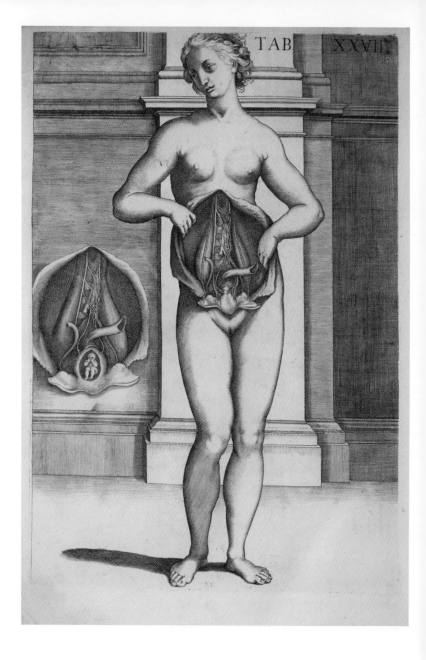

Fig. 2
Female figure, from Gaetano
Petrioli, *Tabulae anatomicae,*
1741

infrequently deploys the term, preferring "culture" and "style" to "taste" and "fashion" as concepts immune from the idiosyncratic and subjective. But the term "taste" was not always thus shunned, and the great debates over the character and universality of taste that characterized the eighteenth century were anything but frivolous. Instead, they were understood as foundational not only for aesthetics, but also for moral philosophy: if a philosophy of taste could be established that bound mortals to a common standard of beauty without resort to coercive arguments, then so too could a code of ethical law. Taste was at the heart of civil society.

For taste to function as a vehicle for social cohesion, it had to be argued that individual judgments concerning beauty could enjoy collective consensus, that they could be both individual and universal. The most well-known articulation of this problem is Immanuel Kant's famous antinomy which states that aesthetic judgments are subjective yet command universal consent. The statement "I walked in beauty" is unlike, and intentionally unlike, the statement "I walked in what I take to be beauty." The former evokes a universally valid subjective judgment; the latter just a statement of preference. For much of Kant's generation of thinkers, a judgment of aesthetic value was not all that distinct from other judgments of taste, such as a judgment regarding sweetness versus bitterness, except the metric for aesthetic judgments was the sensation of pleasure and displeasure rather than excitation of the taste buds. As Kant writes: "if we then call the object beautiful, we believe we have a universal voice and lay claim to the agreement of everyone...."[16]

But who is this "everyone"? As J. M. Bernstein discusses in this collection, Kant's controversial claim was that every judgment of taste calls into existence at least the possibility of a common community rendering similar judgment. Every judgment of taste presumes the existence of a community of sense, a common sense, a *sensus communis*. Membership in the *sensus communis* may not be easy to identify; in fact the aesthetic community may not even actually exist. But the act of aesthetic judgment presumes its existence.

In a fine article by Finnish sociologist Jukka Gronow, the *sensus communis* is equated not with an identifiable group of people, but with a demand, an idea, a promise that can never, in fact, be realized.[17] She cites Jean-François Lyotard, who refers to the social clustering that emerges around issues of taste as like a horizon or a cloud:

"the kind of consensus implied by such a process…is in no way argumentative but is rather allusive and elusive, endowed with a special way of being alive…always keeping open the issue of whether or not it actually exists. This kind of consensus is definitely nothing but a cloud of community."[18] Such a "republic of taste" has no chance of actual concrete existence as it is always doing and undoing itself, but it is nonetheless the terminus and desired condition expressed in each individual declaration of being in the presence of the beautiful. Undoubtedly, the vigor with which popular media strives to affirm the solidity of communities of taste is evidence of their perceived instability.

It is worth remembering that interior design has a particular purchase on this legacy of calling forth a desired collective through cultivated statements of taste. Certainly the field is aware of this tradition, but it is hardly a source of unambiguous pride. The field's episodic and earnest attempts to selectively distance itself from its own history—to posit a state of affairs "after taste"—are in response to charges of subjectivism, elitism, and classism that cling to the history of eighteenth-century enlightenment itself; who, after all, but wealthy white English gentlemen or German philosophers had the time and comfort to contemplate with utter disinterest objects of beauty in the world? But one could argue otherwise, namely that this philosophical tradition is a profound and revolutionary aesthetic foundation, since it asserts that "the hunger of a king did not, in principle, differ from the hunger of a beggar."[19] The 1709 essay/letter *Sensus Communis: An Essay on the Freedom of Wit and Humour* by Anthony Ashley-Cooper, Third Earl of Shaftesbury, which counts as among the earliest extended efforts to define the term, positioned the *sensus communis* at the very birth of civil society as the self-conscious expression of the natural pleasure of human companionship.[20] The *sensus communis* is nothing less than the "sense of partnership with Human Kind."[21]

We could stop here. But Gronow offers a further elaboration on the *sensus communis* and taste that is worth considering in the context of interior studies. Improbably, intriguingly, she sees judgments of taste and universal communities of sense finding expression in a most transitory of human design enterprises, namely fashion. *Pace* Kant, for whom fashion was little more than social posturing and blind imitation and very remote from the classical and timeless standards of taste that he imagined and championed, fashion can be seen as embodying a human activity that most closely resembles pure aesthetic judgment. Fashion issues forth subjective declarations that demand an imagined common community and the community thus issued forth never materializes but is always present. Like Lyotard's cloud communities, communities of fashion are in a constant state of becoming without ever solidifying. Fashion reconciles the basic antinomy of modern life so poignantly formulated by sociologist Georg Simmel, which bears remarkable similarity to Kant's antinomy itself, in which all men are proclaimed equal, and all men are proclaimed uniquely individual, and neither claim can be proven incorrect. And finally, fashion enters into the world without the faintest trace of expediency, and is apprehended with a disinterest in utility that embodies that form of apprehension reserved by Kant exclusively for objects of aesthetic judgment.[22]

Fashion, of course, is to interior design what style is to architecture (in Adolf Loos's terms, fashion is the ephemeral ballroom gown and style is the timeless tuxedo). Fashion/style form one of those binaries to which I referred earlier that serve to negatively define interior design as not-architecture. But if one accepts that interior design functions similarly to fashion in forming cloud-like communities of shared visions of social life, that interior design serves to define collective standards of taste yet endlessly recedes just as those standards threaten to annihilate individuality and difference, and that its superficiality is the source and site of its durability as a social good, then, with Nietzsche, one can begin to imagine a gay science of appearance in which interior design is a principal agent.

The epigraph to this chapter is from Friedrich Nietzsche, *The Gay Science* (New York: Vintage Books, 1974), 38.

1   Clifford Geertz, *The Interpretation of Cultures: Selected Essays* (New York: Basic Books, 1973), 3–30.

2   Gilbert Ryle, "The Thinking of Thoughts: What Is 'Le Penseur' Doing?" in *Collected Papers*, vol. 2, *Collected Essays, 1929–1968* (New York: Barnes & Noble, 1971).

3   Karl Popper, *The Poverty of Historicism*, as cited in *Karl Popper*, by Bryan Magee (New York: Viking Press, 1973), 30.

4   Carlo Ginzburg, "Morelli, Freud and Sherlock Holmes: Clues and Scientific Method," trans. Anna Davin, *History Workshop*, no. 9 (1980): 5–36.

5   Ibid., 21.

6   Edgar Wind, *Art and Anarchy* (London: Faber & Faber, 1963), 41.

7   Freud quoted in Ginzburg, "Morelli, Freud and Sherlock Holmes," 10.

8   Ginzburg, "Morelli, Freud and Sherlock Holmes," 21.

9   Ibid., 22. See also note 67 in Ginzburg.

10 Sister Parish, Albert Hadley, and Christopher Petkanas, *Parish Hadley: Sixty Years of American Design* (New York: Little, Brown, 1995), 98.

11 Gustave Flaubert, *Madame Bovary*, Oxford World's Classics, trans. Margaret Mauldon (Oxford: Oxford University Press, 2004), 31.

12 Larissa Bonafanta, "Nudity as Costume in Classical Greek Art," *American Journal of Archaeology* 93, no. 4 (1989): 543.

13 Alexandra Warwick and Dani Cavailaro, *Fashioning the Frame: Boundaries, Dress and the Body* (Oxford: Berg, 1998), xvii.

14 Claudia Benthien, *Skin: On the Cultural Border between Self and the World*, trans. Thomas Dunlap (New York: Columbia University Press, 2002).

15 Ibid., 87.

16 Immanuel Kant, *Critique of Judgment*, trans. Werner S. Pluhar (Indianapolis, IN: Hackett Publishing, 1987), 54.

17 Jukka Gronow, "The Social Function of Taste," *Acta Sociologica* 36, no. 2 (1993): 93.

18 Jean-François Lyotard, *Peregrinations: Law, Form, Event* (New York: Columbia University Press, 1988), 38.

19 Gronow, "The Social Function of Taste," 92.

20 Anthony Ashley Cooper, *Sensus Communis: An Essay on the Freedom of Wit and Humour* (London, 1709), 72. See also John Schaeffer, *Sensus Communis: Vico, Rhetoric, and the Limits of Relativism* (Durham, NC: Duke University Press, 1990), 42.

21 Schaeffer, *Sensus Communis*, 42.

22 Georg Simmel, "Fashion," *The American Journal of Sociology* 62, no. 6 (1957): 543. The point is formulated succinctly in Gronow, "The Social Function of Taste," 90.

TASTY: ON THE AESTHETIC AND ETHICAL UNIVERSALITY OF WHAT CANNOT BE PROVED

J. M. Bernstein

If taste were what skeptics and detractors think it must be, then schools of design would soon become the Bear Stearns of academic institutions, so overridden with toxic cognitive debts that they would need to be absorbed by institutions with more intellectual capital. But since at least 1790—the year of publication of Immanuel Kant's *Critique of Judgment*—there has emerged a painful, grudging, and routinely withdrawn acknowledgment that determining what is true or false (the business of knowledge) and what ought to be done (the business of morality) are not the sole functions of cognition. Even with its fetishistic attachment to the hardness of science, Kant's defense of the objectivity of judgments of taste haunts contemporary philosophy since it does something a good deal more radical than demonstrating how what cannot be proved can nonetheless be objective. Kant's argument works by showing how the conceptual hardness of mathematics and scientific reason depends upon and so presupposes the nonconceptual, noncoercive softness of taste—what Kant calls aesthetic reflective judgment. Needless to say, my contrast between the conceptually "hard" and the nonconceptual "soft" is meant to signal that there is a deep gender subtext to the continual repudiation of taste.

My comments will have two parts: a sketch of Kant's vindication of taste, and a small argumentative arabesque around Elaine Scarry's analysis of artifacts. What will join Kant and Scarry is their belief that aesthetic reflective judgment underlies basic forms of human practice. Taste, construed in the manner Kant recommends, becomes the condition for encountering and constructing a human world at all.

THE REASON OF BEAUTY

A judgment of taste can be *pure*—just an aesthetic matter with no admixture of function or utility or knowledge or morality—only if in our judging we do not consider the object under the concept of what it truly is or is meant to be. Aesthetic judgments are nonconceptual; hence, even when we have knowledge of the object (for instance, if it is a tulip we are perceiving), aesthetic reflective judging requires that we abstract from that knowledge. In order to underline this thought, Kant isolates what he calls "free beauties" as the exemplary objects of pure judgments of taste, those that do not "presuppose a concept of what the object is [meant] to be."[1] Notoriously, Kant's examples of free beauties, things we like "freely and on their own account," are not works of high art but decorative motifs ("designs *à la grecque*, the foliage on borders or on wallpaper, etc."), which mean nothing on their own: "they represent nothing, no object under a determinate concept, and are free beauties."[2] In short, Kant uses the model of purely decorative interior design in order to think about the meaning of beauty as such—a model, we should recall, that made his aesthetics the ideal articulation for the great moment of American nonrepresentational art, namely abstract expressionism. In his Bennington lectures, art critic Clement Greenberg revealed himself as an unreconstructed Kantian for just these formalist reasons.[3] Indeed, we can press the connection between exemplary beauty, the decorative, and high modernism one step further by recalling that it was central to Matisse's modernism that what had been previously repudiated as decorative was to become the paradigmatic for high modernism.[4] Modernism and the objectivity of decorative design survive or fall together—with Kant.

Kant's instancing of the decorative is not a sign, as it is sometimes asserted, of his philistinism, his ignorance of great art, or his appalling taste, even if all those claims about him were true. On the contrary, he argues explicitly for the primacy of design: "In painting, in sculpture, indeed in all the visual arts, including architecture and horticulture insofar as they are fine arts, *design* is what is essential: in design the basis for any involvement of taste is not what gratifies us in sensation, but merely what we like because of its form."[5] That form is not reducible to simple sensation, or to what can be grasped conceptually, is the heartbeat of Kant's aesthetic theory, the purpose for his focusing in on "designs *à la grecque*...." His idea of aesthetic form means to capture a feature of empirical experience of a certain kind—aesthetic experience—that, like Matisse's notion of the arabesque, brings into view the qualitative attributes of, for example, lines having a particular sense of movement and flow that is not reducible to what can be conceptually stated about them. The temptation is to suppose that if what is at issue is not conceptual and thereby not a matter of observable fact, then it must be subjective, in the pejorative sense of that term. It is just this that Kant disputes.

Let me attempt to extract Kant's central thought by beginning with what he calls the "Antinomy of Taste." Here it is in his words:

(1) Thesis: A judgment of taste is not based on concepts; for otherwise one could dispute about it (decide by means of proofs).

(2) Antithesis: A judgment of taste is based on concepts; for otherwise, regardless of the variation among [such judgments], one could not even so much as quarrel about them (lay claim to other people's necessary assent to one's judgment).[6]

At the center of the antinomy—and what falsifies both thesis and antithesis—is the prejudice that blinds us to taste, namely, if a judgment cannot be conceptually demonstrated, if there is no *coercive* proof, then a true argument is impossible. And if this were so, then each of us would be entitled to our own taste, and our subjective determination of what was tasty or not would be final. To quarrel is, Kant asserts, "to lay claim to other people's *necessary* assent."[7] Of course, there are ranges of experience that really are about subjective preference only: I like things vanilla, you like things chocolate—and there's the end of the matter. But the grammar of taste is not like this.

Kant says that judgments of taste of the form "This is beautiful" are reflective assertions of the pleasure one takes in particular objects or states of affairs that, without the mediation of concepts, lay claim to intersubjective validity. Reflective judgments of taste, Kant contends, "demand" or "exact" agreement from everyone, and everyone "ought" to give the object in question approval and pronounce it beautiful.[8] However, since there is no fact of the matter (seeing something as beautiful is not like seeing it as red or triangular), and there is no universal principle (seeing something as beautiful is not demanded in the way that respecting others is demanded by morality), then the aesthetic "ought" is not an ideal prediction of what others will experience, nor a statement of fact to which they must assent on pain of not being one of us at all, nor a moral obligation deriving from an antecedent principle.

Despite lacking the capacity of proof, aesthetic arguments are not mere rhetorical jostling, mere assertions of private pleasure as if an objective truth, not a game of persuasion. Judgments of taste are subject to argumentative support and critical rebuttal. For example, I say that I found his playing beautiful. You respond aghast, urging against me that the playing showed no sense of line, no idea of structure, no view of what the music was about. It was the playing of an impressive colorist, no more. How might I respond? I could respond in kind, pointing to aspects of the playing that I took to express sensitivity to line and structure; or I could complain that what you call colorist playing I think of as romantic sweep. Substantive argument—and not simply rhetorical head butting—is possible. And in such debate, the stakes could be inordinately high; we could be arguing over how best to interpret the achievement of a particular composer, and therefore what the authority of a certain type of musical structure comes to. All this seems to belong to the possibilities of serious critical discourse, despite the inability of either of us to *prove* our case.

Hence, if I in fact went on to say, "Well, I liked it," I would be backing off from my original claim that the playing was beautiful, a claim which means to reflectively raise my pleasure in the playing to an enjoyment I take to be fitting or appropriate or deserved by the object and so demanded of everyone. If I resort to "Well, I liked it," then I am *retreating* to personal taste, as if the playing were like ice cream (vanilla or chocolate). Anyone hearing that phrasing would take the "I like it" statement as a retreat from the "It's beautiful" statement, revealing the utterly different grammars and requirements of the expressions. The withdrawal here is in aesthetics, similar to what the change from "It's red" to "Well, it looks red to me" is in the area of perception. We have a sense of the significance of reflective judgments of taste just in case we hear in the "Well, I liked it" a retreat, just in case the issuing of the statement of mere preference is heard as a way of removing engagement with either the object or you, and so a collapsing into subjectivity: walking away.

Judgments of taste claim objectivity, they aim to speak with a "universal voice," for everyone, and therefore demand that others see things in the same way.[9] Because there are no ultimate grounds for judgment, then retreat is possible; because retreat is possible, the judgments themselves may appear somehow systematically vulnerable; and because they are vulnerable then they are not really objective but merely psychological. Thus it is not an accident that aesthetic judgments have been misrecognized as being merely psychological in character: their form of universality, in its inability to prove itself, makes them vulnerable to this form of dismissal. Conversely, the import of such judgments is proportional; it is because such claims are universal, but are incapable of proof, that they have the relevance they do. How might that be?

Substantive aesthetic arguments are possible. I can give reasons for my claim, offer evidence, provide analogies from like cases, construct a narrative linking the work under consideration to what preceded it, and so try to make its features more intelligible. These structures of support are not simple auxiliaries to aesthetic judgments; part of what constitutes aesthetic judgments is that they are subject to distinct patterns of support, refutation, affirmation, and dismissal, and that without these, without the relevant body of criticism, interpretation, and history, aesthetic discourse and judgment would be impossible (unrecognizable). The rub here is that apparently valid lines of argument do not entail or compel the conclusion, "This is beautiful." It is this detachment that can make the judgment itself look logically disconnected from what supports it, and thus appear to be merely psychological, as if all the arguing were just trying to get you to feel a certain way. Which is half right; the critic does want you to have a certain sensed/sensory/feeling *response* to the object, but it should be, fully and properly, a response to the *object*, called down by appropriate sensitivity and/or cognitive alertness to what is there—which is what all the argument, interpretation, and criticism is about.

In matters aesthetic, American philosopher Stanley Cavell comments, "The problem of the critic, as of the artist, is not to discount his subjectivity, but to include it; not to overcome it in agreement, but to master it in exemplary ways. Then his work outlasts the fashions and arguments of a particular age. That is the beauty of it."[10] In science, in philosophy, and in all those forms of discourse that take scientific reasoning as their model, agreement is achieved by overcoming and so discounting any and all subjective sources of interference. In the arts and in criticism about the arts, the ambition is different; it is to latch on to those features of the material environment to which a sensory response is the only one available but which are nonetheless capable of being non-accidentally shared, shareable because of their rightness, so to speak. Thus, the reason why there is a dislocation between patterns of support and convergence in a conclusion upon which all can agree in aesthetic matters is that the structure of empirical features constituting the object judged—its being composed of just these sounds or just those shapes and colors in that sequence—is also, at the same time, a structure or order or logic of feeling that demands or calls for a certain (sensuous) response in the perceiver. So works of art, things designed in the mastering and including of subjectivity in their construction of an empirical whole, are aligning how things are with how they are meant to strike one, how we feel in knowing them with what we know in feeling them. Because feeling here is neither simply or immediately causally triggered, like the taste of vanilla, nor mediated by a concept, like the empirical features of the object ("This is red"), but a constructed and orderly feature of the object that calls for a sensuous response of a certain kind, then there is the gap, between pattern and agreement, that permits the retreat into mere preference.

Without denying the role of history and culture, what makes Kant suppose that, in principle, our aesthetic responses are shareable? In broad terms, Kant's answer turns on the claim that aesthetic reflective judgments depend on just those features of subjectivity that underlie and make possible objective judgments of matter of fact. Hence, the argument runs, since we know that judgments of fact are shareable, then the subjective conditions underlying them must also be shareable. In order to motivate this thesis, consider occasions of concept acquisition, or those where we are encountering a wholly novel phenomenon, or where we are required to extend a familiar concept to novel circumstances. In each of these cases, what is demanded of us is that we bring the complexity of the phenomenon being encountered into some rough form of unity—making a whole of the diverse parts perceived—in a manner suitable for conceptualization. Therefore, in these circumstances we are experiencing the world in a way suitable for cognitive purposes without the governance of any existing concepts. But this entails that cognition presupposes that we can make nonconceptual sense of our experience, find a kind of sensory order that anticipates what will qualify for conceptual articulation without yet possessing the requisite concept. Our capacity for reflective judging of this kind involves bringing the faculty of imagination (which is Kant's name for the faculty of purely sensory apprehension) into harmony with the needs of the understanding (Kant's name for the faculty of concepts). Reflective judging, in a wide respect, refers to our ability to grasp sensory presentations for which we presently lack the conceptual resources to make sense of. Aesthetic reflective judgment mobilizes the very same wide capacity for reflective judgment under conditions in which the purpose of conceptualization is abandoned.

In slightly more precise terms, Kant is arguing that in order for us to encounter the world at all, in order for any object to appear intelligible to us, it must appear as a unity of the diverse, which, from the side of the judging subject, is equivalent to what allows our sensory capacities (as organized through the imagination) to engage with our intellectual capacities "in general."[11] The idea behind "in general" is that objects and relationships between objects, in order to be suitable for cognition, must appear sensuously in means appropriate for conceptual unification even when no particular concept is at issue or being sought after. This is what it means to attend to the pure form of an object. Thus, what is at stake in aesthetic reflective judgments is the way our sensory capacities are attuned to worldly forms and designs in a manner ideally suited for conceptual comprehension, independently of the actuality of any such comprehension. Kant's way of making this thesis explicit is to argue that aesthetic reflective judgments regard objects as purposive, possessing internal complexity and order, but without there being any actual external purpose, so appearing as meaning-like but without any explicit meaning being offered.[12] The experience of aesthetic judgment elicits and isolates the subjective conditions for objective judgment in general; and because we can share the latter, then necessarily we must be able to share the former. That is what licenses us in demanding agreement of everyone; we all must share the same general capacities for judgment. Not for nothing does Kant label this shared subjective capacity for judgment our *sensus communis*. We are, presumptively, a community of taste or we are no community at all.

Kant does not suppose that because judgments of taste are grammatically normative and universal that mistakes are not made, and that actually coming to share in such judgments is easy or that different communities will initially find different ranges of objects exemplary of what is beautiful. That is why aesthetic and critical discourses matter, and why, for example, most ranges of aesthetic practice lean heavily on classics or a canon in order to support the effort of creating a communal sense, and that once created it becomes difficult to see why other communities fail to agree. None of that difficulty, variation, or apparent relativity shows that the relevant judgments are not, for all that, fully objective judgments everyone ought to share.

ARTIFACTS AND REFLECTIVE JUDGMENTS OF TASTE

However important one might consider art and decoration, to possess a *sensus communis* runs deeper than this. Our capacity for taste, for the most part, works on the objects of everyday experience—the interiors we inhabit and the exteriors that house those interiors—what Kant calls "dependent beauties."[13] Of course, the artifacts composing our interiors when not decorative are functional, and thus Kant assumes that with respect to dependent beauties our aesthetic judgments must track the purposes the object is designed to serve. But what do we mean by functionality? What is an artifact? A use item?

My premise here is that function relates to need, and need relates to the demands of the human body. Hence, the body makes an obvious starting place for interrogating the nature of artifacts. I take the primary feature of the human body to be its hurtability, its vulnerability, its endless capacity for pain and suffering. It is, I think, no accident that the capacity for feeling pain is routinely taken as a criterion for sentience. Because, phenomenologically, the primary feature of pain is its aversiveness, its being *against*. The experiential quality of pain is its awfulness; biologically, that awfulness has the function of signaling to an organism that it is under attack and thus must take appropriate remedial action. A way of phrasing the unity of the experiential and the functional is to say that, all other things being equal, pain necessarily invokes the wish for it to be gone. In her book *The Body in Pain*, Elaine Scarry plausibly argues that what holds for the sufferer must equally hold for the onlooker; to perceive another in pain is necessarily to wish it to be gone, because that is what pain means, even, indeed especially, when that meaning is refused or inverted. For Scarry, these facts of perception must shape our understanding of human artifice since the made world is made in response to the constitutive features of human sentience.

Her account has three levels. First, most broadly, we anthropomorphize artifacts as containing the feeling knowledge of the human body that their functional structure is a response to: "A chair, as though it were itself put in pain, as though it knew from the inside the problem of body weight, will only then accommodate and eliminate the problem."[14] Second, the knowledge the chair possesses incorporates the compassionate feeling of the wishing to be gone that is a necessary component of the perception of another's pain. More precisely, if we visualize the motions involved in the act of making a chair, we would see, Scarry says, "the structure of the act of perception

50   J. M. BERNSTEIN

visibly enacted. What was originally an invisible act of consciousness (compassion) has now been translated into...a willed series of successive actions, as if it were a dance, a dance entitled 'body weight be gone.'"[15] Recall now that aesthetic reflective judging is an effort of harmonizing form and feeling. Thus it seems right to urge that the imaginative "dance" of chair making, which turns invisible consciousness into visible action, to be a work of reflective judging. Creating without an antecedent model, it is an effort that, above all, requires taste. Taste, again, being judgment without determining rules. Finally, "the chair itself memorializes the dance, endures through time."[16] The chair is compassion made effective, indeed, made into a thing.

This should make perspicuous what I have been hinting at throughout: *pace* Kant, reflective judging is a work of nondiscursive cognition, feeling cognition, cognition affectively contoured at each moment, but cognition nonetheless. Taste is knowledge; it is knowledge of sensuous particulars in their specificity and concreteness.[17] This should be less contestable than it has been since what distinguishes nondiscursive cognition from discursive judgment is that in the making of the former we must be sensuously attuned to the object being judged and our judgment must emphatically depend upon that attunement for its possibility and authority.

If this is even remotely correct, then we can extend Scarry's conclusion one step further. Not only is the chair compassion made materially effective, but, apart from unusual instances, the compassion built into the chair is anonymous: it succors the human body as such, any human body. This is the ethical universalism of the artifact. From this perspective, the design of the ordinary, humdrum chair can be seen as a massive ethical gesture, a massive work of compassion through which we acknowledge the pains and stresses of the weight of the human body, the heavy labor that feet and legs and backs and necks must perform in supporting it, the aches and tribulations to which it is subject, and the need for a steadfast acknowledgment of that labor and pain, the need for relief. It is no accident that when one of the designs that constitute the fabric of everyday life "feels" wrong, there is outrage. That outrage is the flip side of the universal claim that every artifact lodges on behalf of the human.

If Kant is right, then aesthetically every bad design deforms, even severs the bonds that make us a community of sense. If Scarry is right, then ethically every badly designed artifact is a small act of cruelty against sentient humanity.

Kant claims that in our capacity for reason we are like gods and angels; and in our capacity for feeling we are like the brutes. Only in the work of reflective judgment, only in the effort of taste, are we wholly and completely human. There is reason for Kant's tasteful claim.

1   Immanuel Kant, *Critique of Judgment*, trans. Werner S. Pluhar (Indianapolis, IN: Hackett Publishing, 1987), 229. The passage I am elaborating here is central to Kant's argument (and much commented upon). Here it is in full: "Many birds (the parrot, the humming-bird, the bird of paradise and a lot of crustaceans in the sea are [free] beauties themselves [and] belong to no object determined by concepts as to its purpose, but we like them freely and on their own account. Thus designs *à la grecque*, the foliage on borders or on wallpaper, etc., meaning nothing on their own: they represent nothing, no object under a determinate concept, and are free beauties. What we call fantasias in music (namely, music without a topic), indeed all music not set to words, may also be included in the same class."

2   The phrase *à la grecque* arose in the eighteenth century to characterize the classicism in what is now called the Louis XVI style. Stimulated by the excavations at Pompeii, which began around 1748, this style put an end to the style of rococo (*rocaille*) of Louis XV, and flourished from 1760 to 1792.

3   Clement Greenberg, *Homemade Esthetics: Observations on Art and Taste* (New York: Oxford University Press, 1999).

4   For a defense of Matisse's decorative radicalism, see my "In Praise of Pure Violence (Matisse's War)," in *The Life and Death of Images: Ethics and Aesthetics*, ed. Diarmuid Costello and Dominic Willsdon (Ithaca, NY: Cornell University Press, 2008), 37–55.

5   Kant, *Critique of Judgment*, 225.

6   Ibid., 338–39.

7   Emphasis mine.

8   Kant, *Critique of Judgment*, 213, 237.

9   Ibid., 216.

10 Stanley Cavell, "Aesthetic Problems of Modern Philosophy," in *Must We Mean What We Say? A Book of Essays* (Cambridge: Cambridge University Press, 1976), 94.

11 Kant, *Critique of Judgment*, 217–18.

12 Ibid., 221–23. I take the idea of "purposiveness without purpose" as Kant's effort to provide a secular understanding of living nature. That said, purposiveness without purpose is precisely the thought necessary to make sense of the "decorative," what is designed but without function. Purposiveness without purpose is equally the engine making abstract art possible.

13 Ibid., 219. Kant's German term here is *anhängende*, so "adherent" or, as in Pluhar, "accessory."

14   Elaine Scarry, *The Body in Pain: The Making and Unmaking of the World* (New York: Oxford University Press, 1985), 288.

15   Ibid., 290.

16   Ibid., 291.

17   For one of my attempts to demonstrate the possibility and significance of nondiscursive cognition see my *Against Voluptuous Bodies: Late Modernism and the Meaning of Painting* (Stanford, CA: Stanford University Press, 2006).

OUTSIDE IN/INSIDE OUT: A SHORT HISTORY OF (MODERN) INTERIORITY

Anthony Vidler

OUTSIDE/IN

In a conversation, that in its published form lasted all of 127 years, three philosophers of the early Enlightenment, René Descartes, John Locke, and G. W. Leibniz, discussed the nature of the human mind and its ways of understanding. All agreed that the mind might be compared to a dark room. Descartes called it "a chamber"; Locke, "a dark room"; and Leibniz, a "darkened room." All agreed that the reception of ideas and images from the outside was effected through the eyes, and all then advanced the comparison of the mind to a kind of camera obscura—a dark room with a pinhole, projecting images from outside inside. Descartes described this chamber:

> ...a chamber, when, having it completely closed except for a single hole, and having put in front of this hole a glass in the form of a lens, we stretch behind at a specific distance, a white cloth on which the light that comes from the objects outside forms these images. For they say that this chamber represents the eye; this hole, the pupil; this lens, the crystalline humor, or rather, all those parts of the eye which cause some refraction; and this cloth, the interior membrane, which is composed of the extremities of the optic nerve.[1]

The philosopher of reason even went so far as to claim having seen these images on the back of "the eye of a newly deceased man, or for want of that, of an ox," which, when opened up, displayed "in natural perspective all the objects which lie outside it."

Locke, without entering the anatomical argument, nevertheless spoke of external and internal sensations as the "passages of knowledge to the understanding," comparing them to "windows by which light is let into this dark room," that he described as a "closet wholly shut from light, with only some little opening left, to let in external visible resemblances or ideas of things without." Hopefully, he concluded, these pictures would stay in the room in an orderly fashion as objects of understanding.[2]

The objection came from Leibniz. Space, he claimed, was in no way the open and clear emptiness imagined by Descartes and Locke, a void through which images might pass without obstruction to be received on the white sheet of paper in the camera of the mind. Rather "we should think of space as full of matter which is inherently fluid, capable of every sort of division and indeed actually divided and subdivided to infinity." In this ascription, the "dark room" of Locke would already be, so to speak, *filled* with space, and the white screen of Descartes and Locke, no longer a flat, smooth sheet, but always already "diversified by folds" that were formed by innate knowledge, and subject to continuing folding as it received new knowledge from the outside:

> ...this screen, being under tension, has a kind of elasticity or active force, and indeed that it acts (or reacts) in ways that are adapted both to past folds and to new ones coming from impressions of the species. This action would consist in certain vibrations or oscillations, like those we see when a cord under tension is plucked and gives off something of a musical sound. For not only do we receive images and traces in the brain, but we form new ones from them when we bring "complex ideas" to mind; and so the screen which represents our brain must be active and elastic.[3]

And against all three, and in response to Descartes, Blaise Pascal sketched the problem, not as one of interior spatiality, but of the infinite extension of space, and the "horror of the void" it brought with it. His "De l'esprit géométrique" posed, among other questions, an examination of the geometrical understanding of the void.[4] In this brief essay, Pascal pressed the theory of perspectivity to the limits, in an introduction intended for a textbook for the Port Royal "petites écoles." As philosopher Hubert Damisch notes, it was Pascal who drew the conclusion that because "a space can be infinitely extended... it can be infinitely reduced."[5] To illustrate the "paradox" of these two infinities, Pascal gave the example of a ship endlessly drawing near to the vanishing point but never reaching it, thus anticipating the theorem of the geometer Desargues whereby infinity would be inscribed within the finite, contained "within a point," a basic postulate of projective geometry. But whether or not the meeting of parallel lines at infinity would be geometrically verifiable, the "obscurity," as Descartes called it, remained: the ship endlessly disappearing toward the horizon, the horizon point endlessly rising, the ship infinitely close to, and infinitely far from, infinity.[6] Paralleling this discussion, Pascal (or more probably another "Pascalian" author) wrote a short treatise titled *Discours sur les passions de l'amour* in which he linked the sense of the passions to a perspectivity of relations that, when allied to the emerging landscape of boundlessness, resonated throughout the eighteenth century, to be readopted by the situationists in the twentieth.

In this way were formed four of the many theses on interiority that were to emerge during the modern period: the projective and perspectival ocularity that relied on the powers of reason to comprehend the outside world; the systematic organization of knowledge according to a table of associative contents and the organizing power of the mental faculty; the contained and visually occluded comprehension of knowledge sealed within monadic boundaries; and the ultimate loss of all boundaries with the revelation of infinity.

The effects of these and subsequent propositions on the actual architecture of the interior were not immediate; but their effect on the *perceptions* of the interior's power to construct and inform psychic interiority were clear. Sensations, space, and the interaction between the two were constitutive of the human psyche—emotions and rational thought alike were deeply intertwined with the forms of exteriority translated into interior images, thoughts, and ideas.

The ultimate Pascalian landscape was the celebrated Carte de Tendre, fabricated by Mademoiselle de Scudéry in her novel *Clélie*.[7] In this long narrative, forged within a salon circle in the mid-seventeenth century, the narrator, Clélie, was asked how she was able to discriminate among her several lovers, as to who was faithful, who fickle. Clélie accordingly drew a map of a territory she called "Tenderness," and depicted the routes taken by those who were ultimately to be seen as indifferent or faithful. **Fig. 1** The map showed a landscape in sharp oblique perspective, and the three routes to three sites of Tender, each on a river. To the west, the route to "Tender on Gratitude" passed through Kindness, Little Attentions, Assiduity, Willingness, Great Services, Sensibility, Tenderness, Obedience, Constant Friendship; to lose one's way meant falling into Negligence, Inequality, Coolness, Lightness, and Forgetfulness, only to find oneself confronted by the ever-calm Lake Indifference. To the east, the way to "Tender on Esteem" meant surviving Great Effort, Gallant Letter, Love Letter, Sincerity, Big Heartedness, Probity, Generosity, Exactitude, Respect, and Benevolence; to fail led through Pride, Indiscretion, Perfidiousness, Slander-mongering, and Maliciousness,

Fig. 1 (overleaf)
Carte de Tendre, from
Mademoiselle de Scudéry,
Clélie, histoire romaine, 1654

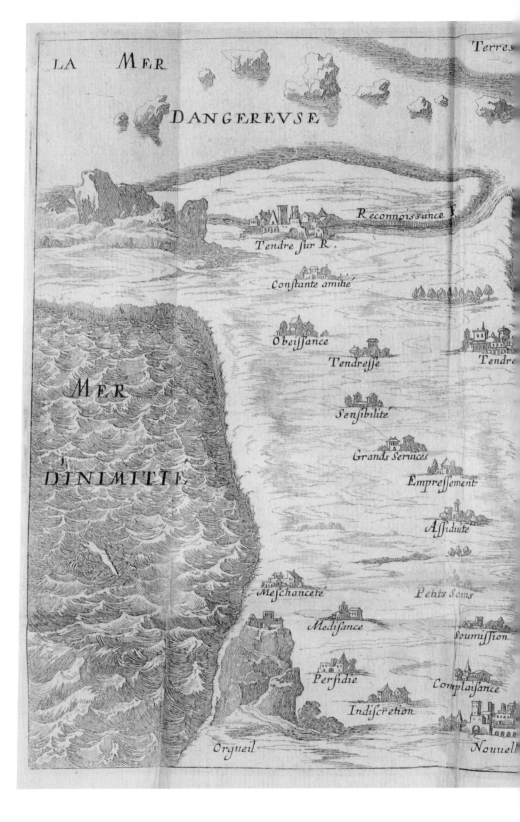

LA MER

DANGEREVSE

Terres

Reconnoissance

Tendre sur R.

Constante amitié

Obeissance

Tendresse

Tendre

MER

D'INIMITIE

Sensibilité

Grands Seruices

Empressement

Assiduité

Meschanceté

Petits Soins

Medisance

Soumission

Perfidie

Complaisance

Indiscretion

Nouuell

Orgueil

ues

Eftime F

Tendre fur L.

Bonte

Respect

Exactitude

Generosite

LAC D'INDIFERENCE

Probité

Grand Cœur

Sincerite

Oubli

Billet doux

Legereté

Billet galant

Tiedeur

Iolis Vers

Inesgalite

and esprit

Negligence

F.C.

| 2 | 4 | 6 | 8 | 10 |

Lieues d'amitie

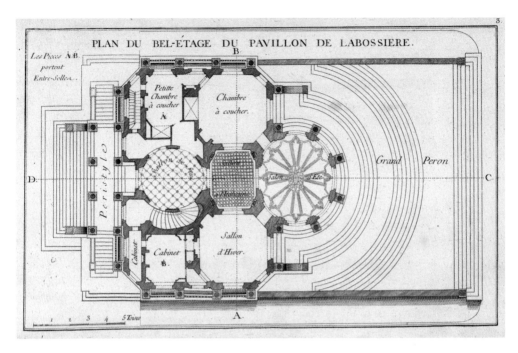

Fig. 2
Plan du Bel-Étage du Pavillon
de la Boissiere, from Georges-
Louis Le Rouge, *Detail des
nouveaux jardins á la mode,*
vol. 1, 1776

arriving at the stormy Sea of Enmity. Finally, the direct route to "Tender on Inclination" passed through the town, quickly reaching the Dangerous Sea, and beyond, the unmappable Unknown Lands. Popular after the first publication, the Carte de Tendre was even taken up as a board game in the mid-eighteenth century.

And if mapping of the soul was an effect of projection into an exterior world that was also the wellspring of ideas and sentiments, then it was not long before the interior itself, no longer privileged as an analog of "mind," took on the role of a passionate interlocutor. Perhaps the most direct exploration of interior architecture as a "discourse of the passions of love" was the novel by Jean-François de Bastide—writer and architectural critic of the mid-eighteenth century—whose narrative of "seduction through architecture" took on all the techniques of display as weapons in the mastery of the erotic arts.[8]

In Bastide's novella, written around 1750, and significantly titled *La petite maison*, or *The Little House*—"petite maison" in French was also a code word for brothels—the narrative centered on the attempt by the Marquis de Trémicour to seduce the unseducible Mélite, who herself was a little bit of a coquette, but, wisely enough, totally "resistant" to the Marquis's advances. As a last resort the Marquis made a bet: that solely through the display of his wonderfully appointed little house could he seduce her. She took the bet, knowing that she was completely unmovable, and especially unmovable by architecture.

The Marquis's "little house" was in fact a very common building type in the eighteenth century; a simple, cubic, garden pavilion of classical proportions with formal/informal gardens and axial routes. **Fig. 2** Bastide had the Marquis lead his victim through the outdoor and indoor spaces of the house, each one more delightfully decorated than the next, showing her first a salon opening onto the garden, "its finery unequalled in all the universe," whose "very voluptuousness" inspired the "most tender feelings," with its painted walls, domes, and candelabras brilliantly reflecting the surrounding mirrors, a salon that was the very image of desire. From there he led her to a bedroom, decorated in *chinoiserie*, with Peking silks, soft yellow tones, and on the ceiling a painting of Hercules awakened by the god of love. Mélite now began to fear her own emotions. But he led her on into a boudoir, the walls of which were sculpted with the trunks of trees, garlanded with flowers and leaves, and hung with chandeliers.

"So magic," Bastide writes, "was this optical effect that the boudoir would have been mistaken for a natural wood."

Mélite's desire was now intense. "Her tongue was mute, but her heart beat fast." Tricking her with hidden music, the Marquis showed her into a bathroom, closing the door behind them without her knowing. Here nothing was spared—marble, porcelain, paneling, walls with arabesques of pagodas, shells and seashore motifs, furnished with a bathtub on one side and a bed on the other. Beyond the bathroom was a dressing room decorated as if a painted birdcage filled with flowers. Mélite now felt weak. "I cannot take this any longer," she cried. "This house is too beautiful, nothing comparable on earth," almost seduced by the spectacle of a bathroom, a function that in the mid-eighteenth century was both new, and an object of fashionable envy.

But there was more: the culmination of the tour was a room that adjoined the bathroom, with basins of marble and fragrant wood paneling, with curved ceilings open to the sky, with birds in flight. This was the water closet, an even newer function for the house than the bathroom. Beyond this was the wardrobe. And from this, by way of a mysterious mezzanine, Mélite was conducted back to the salon, with a view of the amphitheatrical garden lit by two thousand candles. Finally, she was led into a small study, a game room filled with exotic furniture and goods from China and the East, and from there into a smaller study reserved for the preparation and enjoyment of coffee—another of the newest luxuries.

The next scene was played out in the dining room, where a secret lift raised up the table settings and food from the kitchens below, allowing the Marquis and Mélite to eat together privately. Finally Mélite, in a flustered condition, stumbles into yet another boudoir, decorated in green silks. Here finally the Marquis announced his love, throwing himself before her on his knees. Shaken with fear, Mélite resisted. "Cruel woman," the Marquis cried, "I shall die at your feet, or I shall obtain what I want." "The threat was terrible, the situation even more so. Mélite shuddered, faltered, sighed, and lost her wager."

Of all the late eighteenth-century architects to have followed this route, from architecture to seduction, Claude-Nicolas Ledoux was the most striking. A student of Bastide's friend, the architect and teacher Jacques-François Blondel, Ledoux's early commissions neatly paralleled the spatial eroticism of the writer. Thus for Madame du

Barry, the latest mistress of King Louis XV, who had superseded the former mistress, Madame de Pompadour, Ledoux built a real *petite maison* on the grounds of Versailles, a retreat in which she might receive her royal lover. The party thrown by the king on the completion of the house in 1771—the housewarming party, as it were—seemed, as recorded at the time, to repeat every one of Bastide's imaginary scenes, with ornate table decorations in the form of temples rising from the kitchens below, an orchestra in the balconies above, and at the center, Madame du Barry and Louis XV.

It was not long before Ledoux gained the reputation of an extravagant but entirely fashionable architect to those who demanded elegant hotels in the new properties opening up to the west of the old center of Paris—the lands now surrounding the Gare Saint Lazare. For Mademoiselle Guimard, the premiere danseuse of the Paris Opera, Ledoux built another little pavilion, that he called the Pavilion of Terpsichore, muse of the dance; here the rites of Bacchic dance were celebrated in the sculpted motifs above the entrance, and more literally in the small private theater above the carriage house. Bastide's narrative was repeated once more in the movement from the main room to the oval salon, the anteroom to the dining room, the dining room itself, and behind to the boudoirs, and thence around a courtyard to the private apartments. The dining room with its anteroom and skylights and mirrored walls was the pièce de resistance, with the light falling from a skylight above and mirrors painted with images of trees forming a kind of reflected forest. **Fig. 3** While dining, the guests were, so to speak, seated in a clearing, bounded by a forest, which was multiplied to infinity in the mirrors. And then after dining, the guests would pass to Mademoiselle Guimard's little theater, in order to view the kinds of performances that local critics said were only fit for the eyes of voyeurs.

Between the 1770s and his death, Ledoux was to elaborate these fantasies in a series of projects for a new, ideal town, associated with the building of a saltworks near the forest of Chaux in Franche-Comté. This town, appropriately enough sited in a river valley popularly known as the Val d'Amour, was to become the object of Ledoux's obsession for his entire life. It was finally published two years before his death in a didactic treatise titled "Architecture Considered in Relation to Art, Mores, and Legislation" (*Architecture considérée sous le rapport de l'art, des moeurs et de la legislation*), a work which, according to a close friend of the architect, was based on Ledoux's

Coupe

Fig. 3
Section, Claude-Nicolas
Ledoux, Maison Guimard,
1771, from Ledoux,
L'Architecture, ed. Daniel
Ramée, 1849

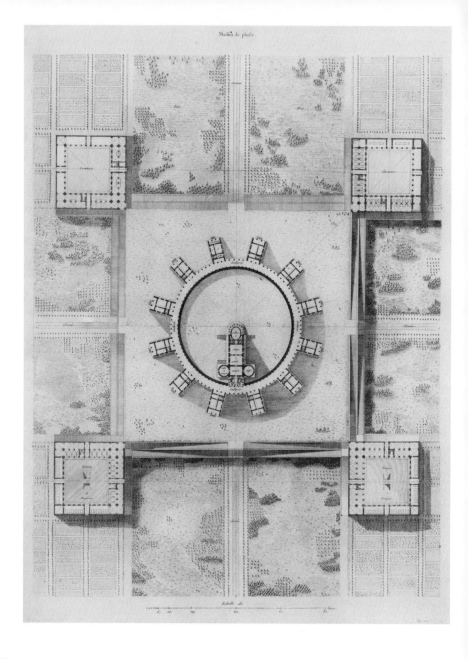

Fig. 4
Plan, Claude-Nicolas Ledoux,
Oikéma, from Ledoux,
L'Architecture, vol. 1, 1804

enthusiastic reading of another erotic novel, the fifteenth-century *Hypnerotomachia Poliphili*. Ledoux's utopia contained designs for many *petites maisons*, most notably one that he dubbed an *Oikéma*, itself the Greek word for "small house," commonly understood to signify a brothel or *maison close*. The function of the *Oikéma* was, with appropriate Enlightenment instrumentalism, more explicit than Bastide's little house. In its institutional form, it was modeled on a number of projects for officially administered brothels in Paris and proposed as hygienic measures by writers such as Rétif de la Bretonne; in Ledoux's text, it took on the air of an Orientalist conceit. In architectural form, however, it took the prevailing notions of character—a building's form should express its use through direct visual means—and propriety—a building should accommodate use in a suitable manner (*caractère* and *convenance*)—to an extreme. Preserving the proprieties in its external guise as seen from the ground as a Greek temple, only in its plan did its role of moral purifier through sexual initiation become clear. **Fig. 4** Its passagelike arcade of bedrooms and alcoves arranged along a second-story gallery leading to an oval garden salon, all surrounded by pools, dining rooms, and dance halls, were combined in an unmistakably phallic plan, recalling the priapic temples engraved by Piranesi on the Campo Marzio, and studied by late eighteenth-century erotic *erudits* like Richard Payne Knight.

Ledoux's little architectural joke, where only the architect himself was privy to the plan and its signification, was perhaps, like Bastide's novella, among the last erotic narratives to preserve the classical *convenances*. Certainly when the Marquis de Sade described the mise-en-scène for the rituals of the *Cent-vingt jours de Sodome*, or when Charles Fourier depicted his new communities of *amour social* in his imagined communities or phalansteries, the fiction of "architecture" as traditionally understood was dropped in favor of an art of the endless, mechanical manipulation of space—a kind of literal parallel to the mechanization of eroticism in their texts through repetition and systematization. Throughout the nineteenth century, and until the invention of psychoanalysis, eroticism was to be obsessed by the material devices of vision, elaborating a kind of voyeuristic mechanics with the aid of shutters, peepholes, projectors, and eventually, cameras. As Michel Foucault has pointed out, there was little difference between the mechanistic structures of a Benthamite Panopticon prison, a hospital, a clinic, an asylum, or even a school. There was likewise to be little room for the secret and arousing chambers of desire in the cool and transparent environments of modernism—if there is a place for the erotic in Le Corbusier's urban utopias, it would be in the suspended fear of the void of infinite space, *l'espace indicible*, and in the pleasure of the superman who overcomes this fear. Banished to the furtive encounter in the marginal spaces of latrine and underpass, modern architectural eroticism, as French playwright Jean Genet understood, was less a question of *convenance* than of its complete demise.

It is clear that the modern interior comes into being with the invention or the development of the self-conscious individual modern subject—the subject that has personal interiority. So it is that we have no interior in the modern sense, until we have an interior subjectivity in the modern sense—that is with the philosophical enquiries of Kant and Rousseau. This is the moment where subjectivities—think of Rousseau's *Confession*, Kant's notion of individual autonomy—come together to describe "being" as a state of attaining personal self-development, and therefore autonomy as an individual.

The form of the interior, as we have seen—its interior narrative, if you will—comes at first from the outside. It was after all from the outside, from the impressions received from external sensations, that knowledge was first identified as having power over the individual. Locke and Leibniz agreed that all knowledge comes from the outside through the sensations, and is transformed, by a kind of trick of the mind, into ideas. The concept of ideas coming from sensations, sensations imprinted on the mind and transformed by the individual subject, came to a head in the narrative structures of exterior environments: wild landscapes and seascapes, urban views treated as landscapes, and exotic views of travel were at once seen as sources of what Edmund Burke called the sublime—feelings of terror and awe—and domesticated as so many "pictures" that might be framed and viewed on walks. The succession of framed views presented to the eye in the landscape garden—as in one of the most notable, Henry Hoare's Stourhead—with each view calculated to give a particular impression or stimulate a memory, literary or pictorial, is understood as the spatialization of narrative; the narrative line is a pathway, and a story is told in pictures through the movement of the viewing subject.

The emergence of the novel, from Daniel Defoe's *Robinson Crusoe* to Laurence Sterne's *Tristram Shandy*, was commensurate with the emergence of the picturesque, and led to experiments in narrative form itself. Thus Sterne in *Tristram Shandy* spatialized his narrative within the book itself. In the original publication of *Tristram Shandy* is the famous quotation, "Alas, poor Yorick" (echoing Shakespeare's *Hamlet*), which is followed by a black page, signifying the completion of the phrase, "he is dead." Or equally, as Uncle Toby talks about freedom, he brandishes his stick in the air and on the ground, and traces a line of freedom. Or even more complicated, and in a diagram that was to be of interest to narratologists in the twentieth century, Sterne, through the voice of Tristram, outlines the different forms of the narrative with linear circumlocutions, now diagrammed within the text. **Fig. 5**

By the end of the eighteenth century, such moves had become commonplace, and architects began to understand spatial sequences in picturesque terms, whether they were exterior or interior. And with the development of the historical consciousness of social development and progress, and the sense of a corresponding progress in stylistic form, builders of Gothic follies and houses, like Henry Hope or William Beckford, traced "historical" paths through their domestic rooms. At the same time, the inventors of new public museums, like Alexander Lenoir in Paris, set up didactic sequences of rooms decorated in period style, often using actual fragments of demolished buildings for added "authenticity" so that the visitor could experience a form of time travel through space. Most extraordinary in this vein are the three row houses in Lincoln's Inn Fields in London transformed by architect and collector John Soane between 1792 and 1837. This vast collection, eclectically assembled fragments of architecture, casts, statues, and pictures, constructed a mise-en-scène that drew the visitor through a sequence of rooms, horizontally as a domestic landscape and vertically through history. From the basement, where Soane installed an Egyptian sarcophagus, a medieval cloister, and a "monk's parlor," through to the upper stories of the dome where he placed the busts of Greek and Roman heroes, this vertical slice, like some archaeological cut, represented the progress of styles from their origins to the present. **Fig. 6**

During the nineteenth century, these interior worlds became more and more privatized. As Walter Benjamin wrote, looking back on the century as a kind of laboratory of modernism, in his evocative unfinished *Passagenwerke* of the late 1920s, "The private individual makes his entry into history."[9] In the new urban pattern, with work and living separated (the shop from the apartment), the sense of a private world

C H A P. XL.

I Am now beginning to get fairly into my work; and by the help of a vegitable diet, with a few of the cold feeds, I make no doubt but I fhall be able to go on with my uncle *Toby*'s ftory, and my own, in a tolerable ftraight line. Now,

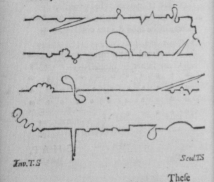

Inv. T.S   *Scul.TS*

Thefe

Thefe were the four lines I moved in through my firft, fecond, third, and fourth volumes.——In the fifth volume I have been very good,——the precife line I have defcribed in it being this :

By which it appears, that except at the curve, marked A. where I took a trip to *Navarre*,—and the indented curve B. which is the fhort airing when I was there with the Lady *Bauffiere* and her page,—I have not taken the leaft frifk of a digreffion, till *John de la Caffe*'s devils led me the round you fee marked D.—for as for *c c c c c* they are nothing but parenthefes, and the common *ins* and *outs* incident to the lives of the great-eft minifters of ftate; and when com-pared

Fig. 5
Laurence Sterne, *The Life and Opinions of Tristram Shandy, Gentleman*, 1760

Fig. 6 (opposite)
Basement of John Soane's
House, Lincoln's Inn Fields,
London. Watercolor by
Joseph Michael Gandy, 1811
Courtesy the Trustees of Sir John
Soane's Museum

Fig. 7
Sasha Stone, Paris interior, ca.
1928. For Walter Benjamin,
the nineteenth-century
interior represented a
phantasmagoria of excess.

protected from the world of commerce develops: the private individual who "in the office has to deal with realities, needs his domestic interior to sustain him in his illusions."[10] This allowed the individual to forget his social functions at home, to leave work behind, and finally to establish a private interior that could become a world apart. And "from this," concluded Benjamin, "derive the phantasmagorias of the interior."[11]

For Benjamin, the nineteenth-century interior was a domain of fantasy that responded, through its decoration and the objects collected, to the escapist desires of its inhabitants. The vision of an interior was wrapped, literally and phenomenally in satin and plush, in what he called a phantasmagoria of excess. In the age of velour, objects and inhabitants alike were surrounded by materials that are soft to the touch, materials stroked and fetishized by the hands. **Fig. 7**

"In the interior," wrote Benjamin, "the owner brings together romantic locales and memories of the past. His living room is a box in the theater of the world."[12] In this sense, the true resident of the interior was the collector, for whom all acquired objects were divested of their former use value and endowed with a new kind of aesthetic value, a "connoisseur" value. This then was the age of the private museum established by collectors in their homes, the decors of which become memorials to the travels of their owners. An example is Viollet-le-Duc's house for the adventurer, explorer, politician, and astronomical scientist Antoine d'Abbadie, a house that is a scientific instrument, compendium of traveler's tales, and domestic interior. Inscribed on the facade are exotic animals from around the world. Inside are d'Abbadie's trophies, ranging from masks to paintings of ritual scenes to a statue of his African servant holding a globe in his hand. The whole is orchestrated with mysterious staircases leading to Moorish rooms, Chinese rooms, Gothic rooms, and scientific observation rooms, replete with beautiful scientific instruments. The entire house is a kind of machine for living in the world out of the world, not exactly a *machine à habiter*, but rather a machine for encompassing an entire lived past.

This mania for collecting, for making the apartment out of the objects that were collected in it and encased by it, this bourgeois "philosophy of the interior" was, as Benjamin noted, gradually erased by the development of modern architecture. Starting with the *Jugendstil* and art nouveau, modernism began to draw in and absorb all the decorative forces that were once dispersed among furnishings, clothing, drapes,

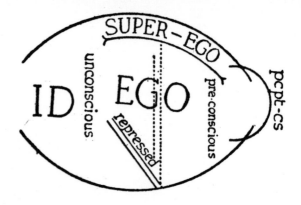

objets trouvés. What was left was a psychic memory, one that demanded to be analyzed as composed of so many layers of forgetting, hidden in the unconscious. Freud's interiors, diagrams of interiority, of the ego and the id, of dreams seen from a bedroom, are diagrams of repressed pasts—diagrams that make of the once cozy interior a site of the "un-homely" or uncanny. **Fig. 8**

These were the repressions that modernism was determined to overcome, whether through the overarching will that drove Nietzsche's superman, or through the technological powers of the new industry. The moment when, as the title of Umberto Boccioni's painting goes, "The noise of the street penetrates the silence of the house," is the moment to flee the house altogether, and rid a new generation of the claustrophobic interiors of its parents. As F. T. Marinetti told it, "Futurism" was born on a morning in 1909, when after a sleepless night, he and his friends took to their newly bought racing cars and drove at speed away from all that their parents represented, only to find themselves overturned in a muddy ditch—a form of rebirth that initiated an avant-garde movement dedicated to power, and the destruction of the old world. But, of course, also the construction of a new world. As Benjamin wrote, "The liquidation of the interior took place during the last years of the nineteenth century." In his terms, the forms of art nouveau, with their iron construction imitating nature, and the invention of reinforced concrete proved "the death knell of the genre."[13]

Fig. 8
Diagram from Sigmund
Freud, *New Introductory*
Lectures on Psychoanalysis,
1932–36

INSIDE/OUT

In a passage that Benjamin quoted, the architectural critic Sigfried Giedion wrote, "Le Corbusier's houses depend on neither spatial nor plastic articulation: the air passes right through them! Air becomes a constitutive factor! What matters therefore is neither spatiality per se, nor plasticity per se, but only relations and interfusion. There is but one indivisible space. The instruments separating inside from outside fall away."[14] Here Giedion was thinking of Le Corbusier's paradigmatic diagram of lived space, the Maison Dom-ino. **Fig. 9** A series of three horizontal slabs raised on pilotis, with no indication of internal or external divisions, this was a polemical attack on the claustrophobic, nineteenth-century interior, now reconfigured as an exterior in order, with the help of a reinforced concrete frame, to bring light, air, and view into the unhealthy enclosures of an earlier era. Pilotis lift the house off the ground, so as to free the ground for the reentry of nature. No longer are windows laboriously pierced through load-bearing walls but now freed to become strips in the thinnest of skins. No longer are the rooms on one floor tied to those on the next for load transmission—the horizontal slab allows for complete freedom on each floor, the free-plan. And the horizontal roof plane allows for nature to assert itself on the roof—a *toit-jardin*. And, as Le Corbusier elaborated the aesthetic of this originally technical invention, these freely distributed surfaces acted as the keys to movement through the house, now envisaged as a promenade through the countryside—a *promenade architecturale*, wending its way through the columns of the house, as if through a landscape that erased the separation between interior and exterior, and dissolving the traditional sequence of spatialized rooms.

Le Corbusier demonstrated this principle in all of his houses and villas, from the little house ("*La petite maison*") that he built for his mother on Lake Leman to the majestic Villa Stein at Garches, or the Villa Savoye at Poissy. The Villa Savoye is, at first sight, simple and clear in its overall form: a cubic volume raised up on pilotis, freestanding in an apparently verdant landscape. Entered from the road by a double driveway, the ground floor is given over to the turning circle of a car, the entrance hall, a three-car garage, and quarters for the domestic servants. A ramp at the center of the square plan leads to the main level, as does a bull-nosed stair. Arriving at the *piano nobile*, the ramp and stair give onto, respectively, the large living room which takes

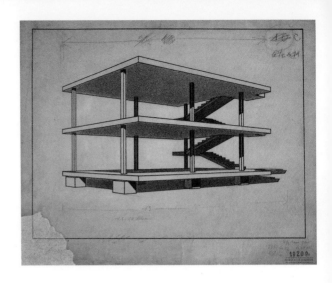

up the entire north side of the villa, and itself gives onto the partially enclosed terrace and the kitchen-bedroom wing, to the east and south. Above, on the third floor, the ramp and stair end in a private solarium, protected to the north and open to the south. We can well imagine how Le Corbusier saw the spaces being pressed into modernist action. After a drive from the Savoye's Paris apartment, the car (perhaps the Delage Grand Sport of Le Corbusier's dreams) swings around beneath the house, stopping with a squeal of brakes to let out its modern passengers, who hardly wait for a moment before jogging gamely up the ramp, pausing to throw off their city clothes in the bathroom, thence out to the terrace to throw themselves in deck chairs, or, more likely, to sprint the last steps of the spiral stair to the solarium, where they might finally throw off the last vestiges of urban civilization, and in true Dionysian fashion, lie naked and browning on their sun mats. The entire house is an aerobic step class in embryo, served by a kitchen as hygienic as a hospital, and a bathroom suite as sybaritic as a spa. Indeed, this was the very image projected by Le Corbusier himself in the movie *L'Architecture d'aujourd'hui*, filmed by Pierre Chenal, where the architect energetically climbs the stairs to the roof garden in the villa of Garches, and a woman actor makes her way up the ramp of the Villa Savoye.

Fig. 9
Le Corbusier, Maison
Dom-ino, 1914
Plan FLC 19209 ©FLC/ARS,
2010. Courtesy the Fondation
Le Corbusier

Le Corbusier was lyrical in his description of the house:

> Site: magnificent property formed of a great pasture and orchard forming a hillock (*coupole*) surrounded by a ring of high trees. The house should not have a front. Situated at the summit of the hill (*coupole*), it should open itself up to the four horizons. The living level, with its suspended garden, is found raised above pilotis so as to allow distant views to the horizon.[15]

The villa has now become a machine to facilitate the view to the outside. We are reminded of Le Corbusier's early drawings of Pompeii and the Acropolis, published in *Esprit Nouveau* and illustrating his twin precepts of the plan: "un plan procède *du dedans au dehors*," and "Le dehors est toujours un dedans."[16] Commentators from Stanislaus von Moos to Beatriz Colomina have noted how, increasingly through the 1920s, this aspect of spatial extension is adumbrated in a number of contexts, from the *petite maison* to the Villa Savoye. Colomina, in particular, has related this move to the influence of photography, seeing the Corbusian villa as a veritable camera obscura, as a machine for capturing the view in its window/lens. **Fig. 10**

Here we are returned to the camera obscura of Descartes, Locke, and Leibniz, but now in absolute reverse: rather than an interior dark room with a single pinhole of

Fig. 10
Le Corbusier, Villa Stein at
Garches, France, 1928
Plan FLC L1(10)65 ©FLC/ARS,
2010. Courtesy the Fondation
Le Corbusier

light projecting the exterior world onto a screen inside, we are presented with an open camera that, as if perversely wishing to develop its film into transparency, projects its interior outside, to the extent that there is no longer any interior or any exterior, but simply what Le Corbusier in his reflections on the Greek space of the Acropolis will call *"espace indicible,"* or "ineffable space."

1   René Descartes, "Optics," *Discourse on Method, Optics, Geometry, and Meteorology,* trans. Paul J. Olscamp (Indianapolis, IN: Bobbs-Merrill, 1965), 91–93.

2   John Locke, *An Essay Concerning Human Understanding,* bk. II, chap. XI, no. 17, (London, 1706).

3   G. W. Leibniz, *New Essays on Human Understanding,* trans. and ed. Peter Remnant and Jonathan Bennett (Cambridge: Cambridge University Press, 1981), 144–45.

4   Blaise Pascal, "De l'esprit géométrique et de l'art de persuader," in *L'Oeuvre de Pascal,* ed. Jacques Chevalier (Paris: Gallimard, Bibliothèque de la Pléiade, 1954), 358–86. This text has been variously dated 1655, 1657, and 1658; recent editors prefer the later dates.

5   Hubert Damisch, *The Origin of Perspective,* trans. John Goodman (Cambridge, MA: MIT Press, 1994), 384–85.

6   Pascal, "De l'esprit géométrique," cited in Damisch, *The Origin of Perspective,* 384–85.

7   Madeleine de Scudéry, *Clélie, histoire romaine: première partie 1654,* ed. Chantal Morlet-Chantalat (Paris: Honoré Champion, 2001).

8   Jean-François de Bastide, *The Little House,* trans. Rodolphe el-Khoury (New York: Princeton Architectural Press, 1996). Originally published as *La petite maison* (Paris: Librairie des Bibliophiles, 1879).

9   Walter Benjamin, "Paris Capital of the Nineteenth Century, Exposé of 1939," in *The Arcades Project,* trans. Howard Eiland and Kevin McLaughlin (Cambridge, MA: Harvard University Press, 1999), 19.

10   Ibid.

11   Ibid.

12   Ibid.

13   Ibid., 20.

14   Sigfried Giedion, *Bauen in Frankreich, Eisen, Eisenbeton* (Leipzig: Klinkhardt & Biermann, 1928), 85, cited in Benjamin, *The Arcades Project,* 423.

15   Le Corbusier and Pierre Jeanneret, *Oeuvre complète de 1910–1929,* vol. 1 (Zurich: Editions Girsberger, 1929), 186.

16   Le Corbusier, *Vers une architecture* (Paris: Les Editions G. Crès et Cie, 1923), 146, 154.

Portfolio: Courtney Smith

Lois Weinthal

Arranging furniture is not a neutral activity. Despite its apparent innocence, furniture arrangement is an act of conquest in which space surrenders its playful adolescence and enters into the rhetorical discipline of the settled domestic interior. The moment a table is placed with four matching chairs arrayed in equal spacing around its perimeter, a powerful domestic narrative fills the room. Indeed the room is no longer any space but becomes its name: "dining room." Furniture marks space, it provides anchor points for a pre-acted and highly nuanced ritual. It matters little if the four chairs are used as projected; furniture well arranged speaks of our social ideals and norms, the equal spacing of identical chairs affirms the perfect harmony and democratic ideal of the modern middle-class family just as the high-backed chair at the head of the nineteenth-century table modeled the ideal of patriarchal hierarchy.

Rearranging furniture, then, can constitute a small rebellion, a tug at the constraints of the domestic scaffolding, even a temporary respite from the tyranny of habit and expectation. But just as readily it can reverse into a reaffirmation of cultural scripture. Yet what if rather than simply repositioning set pieces in space, rearrangement is directed inwardly, to the very syntax of furniture itself? What if the elemental props of the interior refuse to collaborate with the expected silent conformity and assume instead a degree of agency always latent in artifacts so closely associated with the body? Suddenly we are in the realm of material expression of sociocultural critique, or what falls under the rubric of "praxis."

A furniture praxis is a delicate proposition. It entails granting objects license to slit the gauze of routine without tearing the entire storied fabric. Precise cutting is in fact a central metaphor for any design praxis, for incisions across a disciplinary narrative have to be sufficiently penetrating to nudge the viewer into self-critical awareness, yet not so deep as to destroy the coherence of the experience at hand. In the case of furniture, the metaphor can become literal. A cut too deep or imprecise would render the piece functionless (i.e., mere sculpture) and thus ejected from the very drama in which it is an actor.

An example of a furniture praxis is Courtney Smith's *Polly Blue Pell Mell*, in which she dissects a vintage 1950s dresser—that evocative site of personal self-construction, of appearance arranged and rearranged. The piece is cut into discrete fragments, each severed face cosmetically healed with a flawless powder-blue Formica covering. Reassembled in a provisional arrangement (as contingent as fashion itself), the furniture mimics the very act of daily reconstruction that it was originally designed to support.

Smith often explores the characteristics of feminine rooms and furniture in this way, looking, for example, at the boudoir. In *Psiché Complexo* a wardrobe unfolds to reveal a suite of furniture inside. The cuts made to these pieces sever their attachments to the previous owner and assign them a collective identity as an anthropomorphized body. A new personality emerges—at first shy and hidden within its shell, then, when fully extended, becoming comfortable outside of its skin. Unfurled, this boudoir suite reassembles its collapsed form into a new character, and with it, alludes to the possibility of secrets hidden then revealed. Traces of the original intent of the suite manifest as marks left on the surface.

In another example, *Bonito*, Smith carves arabesques into the surface of an existing cabinet. This is not ornamentation, which in its tectonic definition is traditionally deployed to hide a seam or joint. Rather it is a means of producing a seam, of bringing two discourses into dialogue at an edge. As the cuts disclose, the smooth dark wood surface is itself an ornamented field, pale Brazilian peroba wood stained to simulate a richer material, a faux finish masking a plain box that is exposed, not adorned, by the partial field of carvings.

The endgame in this tale of cuts and rearrangements is the actual reversal of subject/object positions. Furniture, as Smith has observed, has a natural tendency toward subject/object ambivalence. In *Lovely Day* a chest of drawers refuses its subservient position along a wall. Drawers open on all sides, displacing the occupant from the center to the margins of the room. It offers no ergonomic concessions: no pulls, no finger holes, no front facade, no backside. It is merely an opaque object lodged, inscrutably, obstinately, in the middle of the room, interrupting the flow of things.

Courtney Smith began her career in Rio de Janeiro, Brazil, where she lived for ten years before relocating to New York in 2000. Smith has exhibited her work throughout the United States, Europe, and Latin America in institutions such as Museu de Arte Moderna-São Paulo; Museu de Arte Moderna-Rio; Museu de Bellas Artes, Buenos Aires; and PS1 and the Museum of Art and Design, New York.

Polly Blue Pell Mell, 2005
Dresser with mirror and two
side tables, plywood, and plastic
laminate
Photographs by Rodrigo Pereda

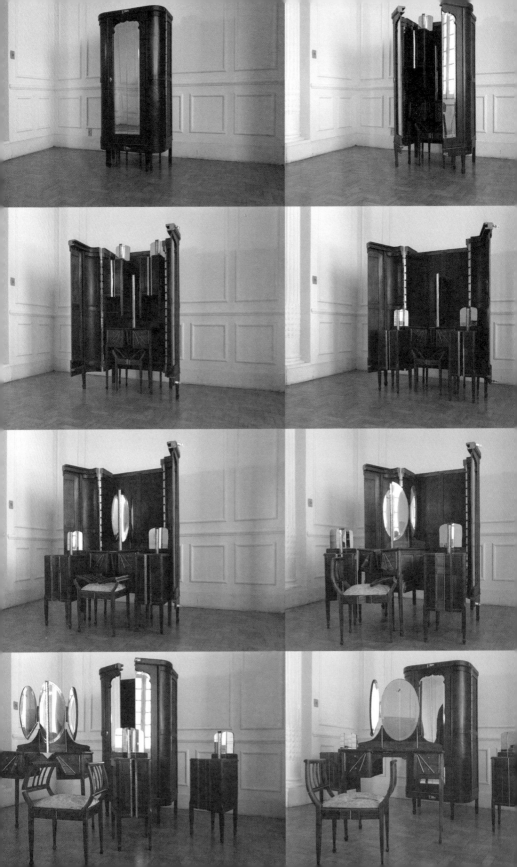

(opposite)
<u>Psichê Complexo</u>, 2003
Armoire, vanity, two side
cabinets, stool with cushion,
hinges, buckles, and hooks
The Speyer Family Collection, New York
Photographs by Fausto Fleury and Vicente
de Mello

<u>Bonito</u>, 2002
Cabinet and hand carving
Collection of Elizabeth Moore, New York
Photograph by Rodrigo Pereda

(opposite)
<u>Gaveta Gato</u>, 2003
Chest of drawers and plywood
Collection of Igor da Costa, New York
Photograph by Fausto Fleury

<u>Santo Antonio</u>, 2003
Chest of drawers and plywood
Photograph by Mauro Restiffe

Psichê Ondulada, 2000
Antique wooden vanity and
mirror, hinges, and assorted
hardware
Collection of Artist Pension Trust
Photographs by Ding Musa

<u>Lovely Day</u>, 2005
Plywood and blue plastic
laminate
Collection of Artist Pension Trust
Photograph by Ding Musa

<u>Homestar</u>, 2004
Vanity table with stool and
plywood
Private collection, Rio de Janeiro
Photograph by Ding Musa

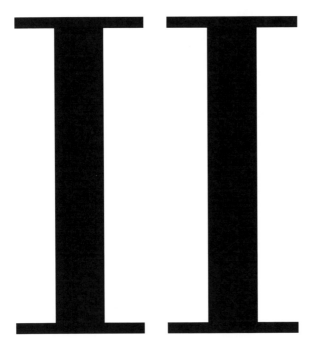

Expanded Pedagogies and Methods

A FOSSICK FOR INTERIOR DESIGN PEDAGOGIES

Julieanna Preston

To propose pedagogy for interior design is an auspicious undertaking. Upon receiving the invitation to compose this essay, I revisited scholarly texts pivotal to my own education such as those by John Dewey, Rudolf Steiner, and Paulo Freire to check that I understood the magnitude and scope of the task at hand.[1] Though I continue to be in awe of such works, any daunting pretensions associated with pedagogy diminished; pedagogy, simply translated, is how and what one teaches, a strategy directed by one's philosophical values. To explore the pedagogy of any creative process, especially a discipline embroiled with professional practice and industry such as design, is a complex charge. Interior design harbors what I consider to be a special set of considerations: it is a subject steeped in the history of the domestic sphere, decoration, upholstery, and home economics and yet it is a contemporary field linking personal lifestyle to the gross national product and international trade. In only a few generations, interior design has shifted from what some would say is a vocational aptitude for the arrangement of home furnishings to a multimillion-dollar-a-year enterprise based on numerous bodies of knowledge and expertise such as building construction, health sciences, environmental psychology, spatial aesthetics, and cultural discourse on space, place, body, and affect. This relatively new and burgeoning design subject is a producer as well as a product of contemporary culture.

Some academics and professional practitioners claim that interior design is in a state of identity crisis. Such claims generally follow the lines of reasoning put forward by C. Thomas Mitchell and Steven M. Rudner: interior design is hampered by general perceptions of "being an 'inferior' design profession to architecture" perhaps promulgated by "...the proliferation of numerous, popular television programs which are labeled as 'interior design,' but are in fact glorified exercises in decorating." Additionally, they point to the "lack of consistent academic standards for interior design graduates entering the profession."[2] John Weigand and Buie Harwood have further noted:

> As it exists today, interior design graduate education is defined by various degrees with different missions, professional content, research content, degree nomenclature, accredited status, credit hour requirements, and curricular focus. This creates a lack of clarity for the consuming public and especially for institutions of higher education.[3]

Shashi Caan, a New York interior designer and educator, adds to the discussions:

> [W]e must quickly strive for a unity of voice and get beyond our self-created confusion pertaining to the core of interior design. We must strive for consensus of the most important and fundamental attributes so that we are in a position of being able to articulate why we do what we do, how we do it and why it is so unique and great.[4]

I propose that interior design's identity is in a state of emergence, not crisis, within the academy and the profession and, most certainly, within public awareness. This state of emergence is predominantly signaled by an international upsurge in new undergraduate and postgraduate programs specific to the discipline, with wide differences in degree nomenclature with equally diverse degree structures, as well as emphases on professional practice and attention to research scholarship. It is underscored by a significant increase in recent years of worldwide conferences, publications, and research initiatives dedicated specifically to interior design issues. From the viewpoint of pedagogy, this essay provides evidence for interior design's emergence and offers some insights into the value of reveling in that state of transition.

As the title of this essay indicates, I will begin with a spatial metaphor. To "fossick" is to rummage, hunt, and search in hope of finding small morsels out of sight, overlooked, or abandoned by others. As an action, fossicking is particularly fitting as an emblem of my search for interior design pedagogy; even the sound of the word infers a scratching through existing terrain—much like the New Zealand kiwi bird, nocturnally foraging the forest floor, fluffing it bit by bit. Fossicking carries a sense of un-doing, re-sorting, and making new ground, figuratively speaking. This metaphor enables interior design's histories and future(s) to be reconsidered and imagined through an active process of iterative searching. Here, I am striving to pay respect to the numerous well-founded interior design programs around the world known for producing quality graduates who become quality practicing professionals no matter what their curricular orientations might be. And, at the same time, I am advocating that interior design revel in becoming as spatially and temporally indeterminate as the metaphor suggests.

What is the nature of the ground that this particular fossick has turned over? Broadly considered, the ground of interior design is constituted by a gritty mixture of unequal and varying portions of embarrassment over and embracement of its origins in the decorative arts; a steaming loam from design's conception as an applied practice and commercial enterprise; a coarse gravel unsettled over its relation to architecture; and a fourth and relatively recent set of air-infused particulates: interior design's engagement with interiority, spatial experience, performance, and temporal inhabitation.

In my opinion, these four conditions form the crux of how, what, and why we teach interior design in the ways we do. Ask any interior design academic about their position on these issues and you will gain insight into the history, technology, theory, or model of studio instruction they practice. It will reveal to some extent how broadly they read, what tools and processes they use to design, and what domain of research they explore most. Because of their proclivity to function as strong pedagogical indicators, these four matters of ground lend structure to my provocation. Ultimately, it is their seemingly very messy, contentious, diverse, and ill-defined nature that underpins my call for dwelling within "inter"-disciplinarity.

Throughout this essay, I have deliberately woven in a varied, divergent, and sometimes discordant collection of voices featured in contemporary discourse on interior design education. Though far from harmonious, the diversity of these voices is a registration of interior design's struggle to emerge as a nonhomogenous discipline and practice.

GRIT

Interior design's relation to interior decoration is well documented. In a body of public and anecdotal discussions that range from scorn and cautiously couched historical respect to positions for and against "curtains and cushions," the discipline of interior design expresses an overall desire to confront and/or transcend the cultural burden and image generated by this heritage.[5] Designer and historian Lucinda Havenhand equates interior designers' rejection of interior decoration with a strategy of androgyny, a form of "otherness." She explains that the field, in the process of trying to gain recognition from a general public (and from government, industry, and universities) that places little value on the irrational and the emotional, has suppressed that feminine aspect of its identity.[6] Further, she remarks that in this marginalized state, "interior design is perceived as feminine, superficial, and mimetic as compared to a male, rational, and original architecture."[7] Referring to design in general, educator Ron Levy questions design's contemporary identity separate from its nineteenth-century origins in upholstery, craft, and the decorative arts: "Design, as a distinct discipline, has rarely sought to develop knowledge constructs within which the activities of thinking, planning, creating and producing artifacts could be shown to be tributary to epistemic principles."[8] On another front, designers Caroline Hill and Carl Matthews belie the conundrum associated with the discipline, its roots, and its gendered identity with a wily question: "What's wrong with pretty?"[9] These examples and others display a willingness to embrace interior decoration as meaningful to interior design's lineage, to revalorize the feminine, and according to Hill and Matthews, to construct the discipline's "cultural dignity and social weight."[10] As feminist scholar Christine Di Stefano notes, interior design may be well served by changing its strategy to a form of antirationalism which "celebrates the designated and feminized irrational, involving a strong notion of difference against gender-neutral pretensions of a rationalist culture that opposes itself to nature, the body, natural contingency, and intuition."[11]

This evidence exposes several points specific to this fossick for interior design pedagogies. On the surface, it reveals a discipline grappling with its roots in the wave of patriarchal modernism, which advanced through industrial progress—a post-arts-and-crafts phenomenon. As a matter of historical narrative, it opens questions as to which stories we teach and how we frame, edit, and critique those stories. It even raises the possibility of reconstructing those stories, which is the essence of theory. Looking a bit deeper, it highlights a range of topics core to other knowledge bodies that, if responsive to my call, interior design educators could link to their curriculum, include in their reading lists, and speak openly about in their design studio critiques. It may serve our discipline well to redirect what has been criticized as a confused, fragmented, and ill-defined identity in order to respond with more authority to issues facing the postindustrial and global communities bound up with political, social, and cultural economies. Such an effort depends on grappling with how matters of decoration, craft and craft technologies, homemaking, home economics, pattern, emotion, psychology, and gender and feminism impact and are impacted by the design of interiors. This response is not made in isolation but necessarily requires pedagogical expansion.

Like all modes of contemporary creative practice including art, architecture, and design at large, interior design is an agent within a broader field of industrial production, consumerism, and lifestyle economies. Enticing criticism as well as advocacy, the consumptive side of interior design is entangled with the practical application of skills, drawing lines between training and education and the role of design in a larger context. This distinction belies interior design education's shift from trade schools to technical colleges and, in the more immediate past, to universities. Speaking to design in general, former co-chair of design at Cranbrook Academy of Art Katherine McCoy calls for design education to extend beyond financial imperatives: "Specialized training is not enough. We must educate our new designers for this larger ethical view if design is to become more than the servant of commercialism."[12] Ron Levy reinforces McCoy's call and suggests that instead of focusing on training in practical skills, "[d]esign schools in a university setting should focus primarily on developing fundamental knowledge and imparting understanding of the process of analysis, synthesis, interpretation, creation, evaluations, and judgment."[13] No longer concerned with seemingly esoteric dimensions of arranging (pretty) things in domestic space, or solely interested in designing accessories for the pleasure of what modern life promises, interior design finds itself in a thrilling yet slightly precarious position: to revamp its liaisons with capitalism. Ron Levy bridges the gap between capitalism and modern life's (and design's) penchant for technological engagement:

> [W]e can observe that, while the design field continues to preoccupy itself with the technicalities of teaching design know-how, the rest of the techno-scientific community is moving rapidly in various directions, regenerating knowledge constructs concerning the paradigm of complexity and even appropriating the concept of design into their own repertoire of representing and reconstructing the world. What if design entertained current debates in the techno-sciences? What would happen if design developed instrumental and existential methodologies around cognition, creation, and production of artifacts? And how would design then consider the being dwelling amongst those artifacts? Then in this

kind of knowledge-based context we would see fundamental changes take place in the learning-processes of designers; this would have far-reaching effects on design practices, design responsibility, and design credibility.[14]

Interior design has the potential to mature beyond its status as an object of cultural criticism and to become a hotbed of innovation that realizes the ethical dimension to commercial enterprise. From a pedagogical perspective, interior design might find fruitful collaboration with disciplines such as information science, robotics, electrical engineering, and digital three-dimensional fabrication and modeling in order to drive technology tactically instead of merely being co-opted by it.[15]

More evidence is found for this approach in a paper by spatial designer and educator Antony Pelosi titled "Interactive Construction Documentation," in which he explores the potential for three-dimensional modeling and four-dimensional simulations as alternatives to conventional construction document representations.[16] He notes the advantages of real-time virtual environments to host such hybrid representations and become accessible to all construction industry stakeholders. His research effectively spatializes a communication process that increases the success rate of completing a job on time, to budget, and with attention to detail—factors significant to the commercial interior design sector. In another example, designer and educator Stuart Foster demonstrates the use of Radio Frequency Identification (RFID) technology to track how inhabitants and objects interface in actual and virtual space even as they change and move over time.[17] With these examples, I am advocating a far more aggressive interaction with technologies that enable interior designers to envision and materialize products, environments, and experiences. As engineering professor Michael Ashby and industrial design educator Kara Johnson predict, "...the twenty-first century will be that of surfaces, mono-layers, even single molecules, and the new functionality that these will allow."[18] How could we not want to be part of this future; to further invest in our discipline's well-developed sensibility around materials, to shift from specification and stylistic application to innovation?

Interior design's relationship to architecture is competitive and contentious in nature. Each maintains a degree of autonomy and distinctiveness based on the scope of services offered in a professional setting, a territorial boundary that is well defended by each entity's allied professional, accrediting, and registration communities. Interpreted by the general public, it would suffice to say that architecture is equated with a physical building structure formally related to its exterior context, whereas the inside of a building is the proper domain of interior design practice. In terms of pedagogy, this seemingly secondary position may be evidence of the power that interior design history and theory reading lists have had in shaping the discipline's identity. For example, in the introduction to *A History of Interior Design*, John Pile writes, "Interiors are an integral part of the structures that contain them—in most cases, buildings. This means that interior design is inextricably linked to architecture and can only be studied within an architectural context."[19] With reference to Elias Cornell's historical summary, "Going Inside Architecture: A Tentative Synopsis for a History of the Interior," Pile starts with the cave as the original interior and traverses the great moments (thus far) of architectural history from the inside and from a tectonic perspective.[20] Furthermore, architecture academic Joy Monice Malnar and fine arts professor Frank Vodvarka articulate the severance of interior from exterior as they proceed to outline the theory of interior design as enclosed space:

> One of the most fundamental divisions in design is that of interior from exterior, volume from mass. As the interior and exterior are perceptually separate, sustaining coherence between them is a difficult task. It entails a significant divergence in design approach, despite many shared theoretical assumptions and techniques. This divergence accounts for two realities: first, from the eighteenth century to now, the design distinction between interior and exterior has tended to sharpen; and second, this is partly the result of a radical alteration in the socioeconomic and technical nature of buildings themselves.[21]

This inside-outside mode of demarcating knowledge bodies and professional services continues to proliferate in discussion, discourse, and pedagogy not only for the convenience of its simplicity, but for the ease at which it reiterates the historiographic patriarchy of architecture with interior design as its lesser, feminine cousin. For example, positioning interior design as a lineal descendant of decoration, Professor of Architecture Innovation and Chair of Design Practice Research Leon van Schaik argues that interior design's role is merely to make buildings inhabitable—an inferior, normative, and socially compliant purpose.[22] Such reasoning posits interior architecture, not interior design, as the natural and rightful partner to architecture and its ability to be exceptional (i.e., to defy the entropic tendencies of social, economic, and ecological systems).[23]

Protagonists of interior architecture such as Fred Scott, Graeme Brooker, and Sally Stone make further claim on the inside of buildings as interior architecture's domain, in particular, the renovation, addition, and adaptive reuse of existing structures.[24] Building on academics John Kurtich and Garrett Eakin's vision of interior architecture as part of architecture's holistic motivations, Henry Hildebrandt, architecture and interior design academic, defines interior architecture as "a descriptive language in which the architectural design or architectural language is seen as a continuation or an extension of the exterior architecture to the inside of the structure in terms of detail, scale/proportion, spatial sequence and other such architectural components."[25] With a mutual reliance on context, interior architecture and architecture demonstrate an allegiance to a design process that seeks to unify material and space through the reduction of abstract ideas coupled with program. Hildebrandt goes further to highlight a profound conceptually based rift between interior design and interior architecture:

> [I]nterior design is grounded in the condition of additive assemblies and separate contracted services. While the design processes of architecture and interior design share the same procedural sequence and a core discipline vocabulary, interior design, both as a discipline and in its product, is (or can be) free of the weight of the architecture. Additive assemblies within the "interior" may establish an independent language...intentionally, conceptually, and contractually removed from the building shell.[26]

Whether in an educational or professional context, interior design's association with architecture necessitates an imperative for students and practitioners to become familiar with a wide scope of building technologies, including materials and systems, structures, physics, health and safety issues, mathematics, and sustainable practices. While this association may lend respect and validation to the discipline and provide interior design with a greater degree of authorship in technology-heavy areas such as acoustics, soundscapes, thermal comfort, internal mechanical services, lighting design, textile design, and material science innovation, it also steers interior design toward an instrumental and objective knowledge base, i.e., problem solving, instead of problem inquiry or problem making.

American interior design educator and former IDEC president Jill Pable makes a plea for integrating subjective modes of knowing into interior design pedagogy, research, and practice, while Australian interior design educator and current chair of IDEA Suzie Attiwill reconsiders interior design as a discipline plagued by a divisive binary that places interior design between excess and austerity and subsequently caught between interior decoration and architecture.[27] Attiwill argues against a divisive Platonic binary that is idealist and essentialist in nature, and for an interior apparent as both physical and psychological space. She brings the same level of inquiry to interior design pedagogy in her essay "What's in a Canon?" which tracks the concept of the canon as a reference to architecture, perhaps an outdated idea that alludes to containing, in the sense of restraining.[28] Noting an architectural canon's penchant to store, propagate, and embody knowledge, Attiwill's argument for and against an interior design canon is derived from the notion that the discipline is distinct from interior architecture. Furthermore she asserts that interior design's experimental nature is not based on a given inside/outside nor limited to an object/artifact practice. She offers instead the idea that any interior design canon would necessitate a shift from a historical model to a model of multiple practices that emphasizes the activities of *making* interiors.

To agree with Attiwill and Pable would mean to form a pedagogical interface between interior design, philosophy, cultural studies, women's studies, and theory associated with psychology. In addition, it would highlight ways of thinking about interiors, as Attiwill does, as "composed of relations, phenomenal and emotive."[29] While critics are cautious about this tactic, in which they see an undermining of the discipline reminiscent of a liberal arts model of education, such an approach would take advantage of the synthetic nature of interior design to address what is always spatial and material, experiential and sensed, and enveloped by time as well as substance.

AIR

A fossick is automatically an air-infusing activity. This fourth type of pedagogical ground is lighter, more ephemeral, more intangible than the other mixtures and draws interior design into what Necdet Teymur, professor of architecture, calls "the im/possible definition of the ubiquitous concept of 'space,'" a concept that "encompasses almost *every-thing*, *every-where* and *every-time*."[30] In this way, interior design finds meaningful alliances with film, digital media, television, theater, performance art, exhibition, installation, virtual gaming environments, and other forms of spatial events that are not entirely bound by finite dimensional building structures but constrained by perceptual awareness, subjectivity, and interpretation.

Not as abstract or as fictional as interior design educator Shashi Caan suggests, these interior practices rely on clients and users, materials and industry, and operate to embellish, elaborate, and comment upon inhabitation at large.[31] More importantly, this new hybrid interior design recognizes what American author Stanley Abercrombie asserts is what draws most interior designers to the profession: "The proliferation of interior designers who treat their profession as 'just another business' is detracting from the value of interior design as an artform. Unlike fine art, interior design is an applied art which cannot ascribe to only aesthetic demands. Technique and experience are important factors in this field of art."[32] Rather than steer our concerns about what is included and excluded from interior design pedagogy back to tired debates about the value and purpose of art and modern distinctions (primarily invoked by higher education) between art and design, instead, consider what van Schaik calls "the art of virtual space."[33]

Complicit with contemporary British social scientist and geographer Doreen Massey's declaration of the primacy of space and its inclusiveness rather than opposition to time, and architectural theorist Adrian Forty's outline of a twentieth-century paradigm shift from concerns of surface and tectonics to those of spatiality, Teymur locates a complex slipperiness that cultivates interior design's emergence and its evasion of (regulatory) definition.[34] Whether one charts the interior via Jean Baudrillard's *System of Objects*, interiority through Elizabeth Grosz's feminist philosophy and Freud's psychoanalytic theory, or interiors by way of Charlotte Perkins Gilman's *Yellow Wallpaper* and Eileen Gray's lacquered furniture, only a highly permeable membrane remains between interior and space. The interior has expanded, like a fossick, through an infusion of air; it is more than an inside, a building, an artifact, a commodity, and more than a stable entity. It evades standing still as simply concrete material stuff organized to supplement living; it is located within the tangibility of lived experience.

COMPOST

The only aspect left to pick through in this fossick is the nature of the freshly jumbled mixture it ferments. As Attiwill states, "This tangle of lines and plethora of ways of thinking about interior design could be understood as confusion and a discipline in crisis, triggering a process of reduction and identification; or alternatively, it could be celebrated as provoking experimental connections and lines of flight."[35] While individually the voices differ in tone and approach, the tenor they strike as a whole is internationally resounding: interior design is not what it once was or was assumed to be. So, while interior design education once may have been grounded by a general art or design degree, geared toward planning and fitting out inhabitable spaces inside buildings, and oriented toward style, taste, and fashioned consumer goods, it currently dons identity variants in the name of spatial design, creative industries, and interior architecture. Each of these variants inflects the emphasis, outlook, and educational lessons of a discipline that, as I have shown, has never been stable, emphatically secure, or exclusively defined on its own terms. Furthermore, interior design graduates (as well as graduates of these variant programs) find that they have an expanded set of valuable skills and modes of thinking transferable to employment opportunities such as event planning, theater and performance design, stage set and costume design, exhibition design, government housing policy, historic preservation, furniture design, and lighting and acoustics. Their expertise extends to the design of a wide range of specialist environments such as schools, health facilities, elderly housing, retail shops, offices, museums and galleries, cultural events, and transport interiors, to name a few. And despite regularly expressed concerns over how to differentiate, standardize, monitor, accredit, and regulate the discipline, each divergent strand supports my assertion that interior design is not singular, homogenous, or easily branded. And hence, its pedagogy should follow suit. As Pable states:

> How interior designers choose to explore, accept, and act on knowledge may also influence and reveal how they see themselves....However, it may be the larger long-simmering debate regarding the nature of knowledge acquisition itself that may be a telling backdrop to these indicators....Comfort in accepting and acting on different types of knowledge may be particularly critical for the interior design profession at this time.[36]

In this essay, I have used the term "discipline" to describe a collection of types of knowledge, skills, challenges, approaches, and communities. Like most professionally bound disciplines, interior design education tends toward the development of expertise or specialism; it is not a generalist subject. In this way, the field has been disciplined, to use the term's other meaning, with a very particular focus, a characteristic that Teymur cites as a territorializing process of inclusion (that which is valued) and exclusion (that which is "othered": deemed outside the domain of the discipline). Within design, that focus has usually been delineated by the object that is designed, e.g., textile design, fashion design, digital media design, product design, transport design, and interior design. Such specialization has spawned many degrees, curriculums, and professional bodies, many of which adopt the same nomenclature and effectively carve up the overall field of design into small kingdoms. Each vies for methods of learning, researching, articulating, and marketing in order to reinforce its distinctiveness. This is consistent with the notion that each discipline adopts or develops pedagogy as a matter of differentiation.

Despite the benefits of specialization, most professional designers will readily admit that in order to address the problems of everyday practice, let alone the extraordinary challenges of world issues, one must necessarily liaise, consult, and collaborate with a wide range of other experts. As Australian academic leaders Jill Franz and Steffen Lehmann state, there is "a growing awareness of the need to look beyond discipline boundaries in order to more effectively address issues involving the design of the built environment; issues associated with a rapidly changing and increasingly technologically complex world."[37] This is the impetus to confront interior design's pedagogical engagement with multi-, cross-, interdisciplinary learning contexts and environments. For the sake of clarity, a multidisciplinary context refers to knowledge shared by more than one discipline in which each is tackling a common challenge using its specialized tool kit—essentially, the whole is the sum of its parts. Crossdisciplinary refers to one discipline using the knowledge set of another, i.e., importation across discipline boundaries. Interdisciplinary refers to a context in which knowledge is extended due to the collective efforts of a group interaction, melding disciplinary expertise into something new, something that exists between the disciplines, sometimes a new discipline. Unlike these three modes, transdisciplinary is an aspiration, not a method, to work using a holistic approach that, while moving between, across, and beyond individual discipline expertise, removes the need for discipline boundaries.

For me, framing interior design education within a design research-centered paradigm of border-crossing activities is a priority. In this way, I am advocating pedagogy that maintains interior design in a continuous emergent state in order to foster an identity that is interdisciplinary in nature. It is the act of fossicking, the repeated tossing things up, the flinging things about, and, especially, the injection of air that characterizes interior design's engagement with the virtuality of technology as well as the virtuality of space. Through this process, design takes flight in the face of normative paradigms of disciplinarity, perhaps even disrupting the practice of pedagogy as a discipline fence post. These imaginations/machinations are only original in that I am drawing interior design into a discourse much broader, far more contentious, and yet far more, fittingly so, spatial. Teymur advocates adopting a new concept of interdisciplinarity which focuses on the gaps between disciplinary boundaries. Like the objects of this fossick, these gaps are the leftover, abandoned, or neglected bits of knowledge that join the inside and the outside of disciplines in a spatial continuum that is all inclusive.

Drawing from Teymur's position on transdisciplinarity: "What kind of knowledge would this simultaneously continuous, fluent, omnipresent and universal phenomenon that is both big and small, thick and thin and confined and infinite be the knowledge of?"[38] The impossibility that any one discipline could manage or contain this knowledge only emphasizes that space is a socially constructed system premised on relations.

By insisting on the insertion of the hyphen, Teymur shifts interdisciplinary to inter-disciplines, a move that adds value to those bits of "other," as he states, "these gaps are neither nothing, nor voids...absences of knowledge, or ignorance...but likely to be either different types of it, or raw ingredients of the knowledges to come."[39] These inter-disciplines are further characterized as having the qualities of interframability, interspatiality, interculturality, interlinguality, interdiscourse, and intermedia. Too extensive to fully elaborate here, Teymur's vision provides a ripe opportunity to draw interior design into the spotlight as an inter-discipline complicit with all the discourses supporting and retorting its marginal, peripheral, supplemental, denigrated, criminal, second-class, impure, and excluded otherness, challenging disciplines (and pedagogy) that remain segregated by the notion and practice of knowledge as owned, demarcated territory. Contrary to "intra," that which lies inside, "inter" capitalizes on that which is between, among, amid, in between, and in the midst of, a spatial distinction that separates the interior as the room with four walls and an interior as the space of relational forces and events. What is at risk to take this new concept of inter-disciplines into our teaching and practice of interior design? Could ours be one of the "other" disciplines that negotiate the gaps? Could interior design become an orchestrator to Teymur's vision of spatial democracy?[40] Is the future of interior design pedagogy grounded in its beautiful messy state of emergence? I think so.

1   John Dewey, *Art as Experience* (New York: Minton, Balch & Company, 1934); Rudolf Steiner, *Intuitive Thinking as a Spiritual Path: The Philosophy of Freedom*, centennial ed., Classics in Anthroposophy, trans. Michael Lipson (Hudon, NY: Anthroposophic Press, 1995). Originally published as *Die Philosophie der Freiheit* (Dornach, Switzerland: Rudolf Steiner Verlag, 1961); Paulo Freire, *Pedagogy of the Oppressed* (1970; repr., London: Penguin, 1996).

2   C. Thomas Mitchell and Steven M. Rudner, "Interior Design's Identity Crisis: Rebranding the Profession," in *Thinking Inside the Box: A Reader in Interiors for the 21st Century*, ed. John Gigli et al. (London: Middlesex University Press, 2007), 69.

3   John Weigand and Buie Harwood, "Defining Graduate Education in Interior Design," *Journal of Interior Design* 2, no. 33 (2007): 3.

4   Shashi Caan, "Consensus or Confusion," in Gigli et al., *Thinking Inside the Box*, 55.

5   Teresa Hoskyns, "Not Cushions and Curtains: Textiles, Architecture and Interiors," in Gigli et al., *Thinking Inside the Box*, 98.

6   Lucinda Kaukas Havenhand, "A View from the Margin: Interior Design," *Design Issues* 4, no. 20 (2004): 32–42.

7   Ibid., 33.

8   Ron Levy, "Design Education: Time to Reflect," *Design Issues: Educating the Designer* 1, no. 7 (1990): 42.

9   Caroline Hill and Carl Matthews, "What's Wrong with Pretty?" *Journal of Interior Design* 3, no. 32 (2007): 11.

10   Julieanna Preston, "Soft Stuff," in *The Sensuous Intellect*, ed. Ross McLeod (Melbourne: RMIT Publishing, 2006), 142–55; Havenhand, "A View from the Margin," 36; Levy, "Design Education," 43.

11   Christine Di Stefano, "Dilemmas of Difference: Feminism, Modernity, and Postmodernism," in *Feminism and Postmodernism*, ed. Linda J. Nicholson (London: Routledge, 1990), 67.

12   Katherine McCoy, "Professional Design Education: An Opinion and a Proposal," *Design Issues* 1, no. 7 (1990): 22.

13   Levy, "Design Education," 44.

14   Ibid., 47.

15   Julieanna Preston, ed., *Interior Atmospheres* (London: Wiley, 2008). This is a theme I have explored further in *Interior Atmospheres*, a publication probing interior environments relative to affect and effect, i.e., experience and technique.

16   Antony Pelosi, "Interactive Construction Documentation," in *Proceedings of Ninth International Conference on Construction Applications of Virtual Reality* (Sydney, Australia: 2009).

17   Stuart Foster, "Being @" (master's thesis, Massey University, 2005).

18 Michael Ashby and Kara Johnson, *Materials and Design: The Art and Science of Material Selection in Product Design* (Oxford: Butterworth-Heinemann, 2002), 10.

19 John Pile, *A History of Interior Design* (London: Laurence King, 2000), 8–9.

20 Elias Cornell, "Going Inside Architecture: A Tentative Synopsis for a History of the Interior," *Architectural History*, no. 40 (1997): 24–63.

21 Joy Monice Malnar and Frank Vodvarka, *The Interior Dimension: A Theoretical Approach to Enclosed Space* (New York: Van Nostrand Reinhold, 1992), xi.

22 Leon van Schaik, "Interior Architecture: The Art of Virtual Space," *The Interior* 3/4, no. 1 (1992): 40.

23 Ibid., 39.

24 Fred Scott, *On Altering Architecture* (London: Routledge, 2008); Graeme Brooker and Sally Stone, *Rereadings: Interior Architecture and the Design Principles of Remodelling Existing Buildings* (London: RIBA Enterprises, 2004).

25 John Kurtich and Garrett Eakin, *Interior Architecture* (New York: Van Nostrand Reinhold, 1993); Henry Hildebrandt, "The Gaps Between Interior Design and Architecture," *Design Intelligence*, March 15, 2004, http://www.di.net/articles/archive/2257/.

26 Ibid.

27 Jill Pable, "Interior Design Identity in the Crossfire: A Call for Renewed Balance in Subjective and Objective Ways of Knowing," *Journal of Interior Design* 2, no. 34 (2009): v–xx; Suzie Attiwill, "Di-vision/Double vision," *IDEA Journal* (2003): 3–10.

28 Suzie Attiwill, "What's in a Canon?" in Gigli et al., *Thinking Inside the Box*, 57–66.

29 Ibid., 63.

30 Necdet Teymur, "Space Between Disciplines," *Critical Studies* 1, no. 20 (2002): 97.

31 Caan, "Consensus or Confusion," in Gigli et al., *Thinking Inside the Box*, 50.

32 Stanley Abercrombie, "The Value of Interior Design," *Interior Design* 3, no. 65 (1994): 1.

33 Van Schaik, "Interior Architecture," 41.

34 Doreen Massey, *For Space* (London: Sage Publications, 2005); Adrian Forty, *Words and Buildings: A Vocabulary of Modern Architecture* (London: Thames & Hudson, 2000).

35 Attiwill, "What's in a Canon?," 63.

36 Pable, "Interior Design Identity in the Crossfire," vi–vii.

37 Jill Franz and Steffen Lehmann, "Side-by-Side: A Pedagogical Basis for (Design) Transdisciplinarity," *IDEA Journal* (2004): 9.

38 Teymur, "Space Between Disciplines," 106.

39 Ibid., 103.

40 Julieanna Preston, "What's at Risk? Concerning Matters of (Interior Design) Disciplinarity," *At Looking into the Modern Interior: History, Theory and Discipline in Education and Practice Symposium*, Interior Design Educator's Council, United States

and Modern Interiors Research Centre, Kingston University, London, 22–23 March 2010, Atlanta, Georgia, USA. (Unpublished.) Here I am reiterating a question I posed recently to an international body of interior designers.

INTERIOR DESIGN AS ENVIRONMENTAL DESIGN: THE PARSONS PROGRAM IN THE 1960s

Joanna Merwood-Salisbury

In April 1965 the graduating students of the interior design department at Parsons School of Design put on an exhibition of their work in their studio space, a converted loft on East Fifty-Fourth Street. The thematic show, called *A Place to Live*, focused on the reform of slum housing and included a reconstruction of a Spanish Harlem tenement. In their institutional version of Marcel Duchamp's *Fountain*, this reconstruction came complete with "a naked tenement toilet. A nearby cubbyhole just large enough for a worn gas stove...strewn with grimy pots and pans, cans and cereal boxes."[1] **Fig. 1** A reviewer for *Interiors* magazine noted the incongruity of the subject matter for Parsons, "that stronghold of elegance...which stands for luxurious, raffiné decor." This show, unlike anything ever before presented by the school, was the public face of a reformed program, reflecting profound changes to the curriculum put in place by faculty members James Howell and Allen Tate in the 1964–65 academic year.

Any contemporary steps toward imagining interior design in an expanded field must take note of this mid-1960s moment. *A Place to Live* reflected a new curriculum, one that broke with the limits of the discipline as it had been traditionally conceived and set out an ambitious agenda of social engagement. Under the leadership of Howell and Tate, students at Parsons were encouraged to think of their work in relation to the emerging discipline of environmental design rather than as the then-current manifestation of the history of decorating. At its most extreme, the controversial new "environmental approach," as it was soon labeled, saw students abandoning their focus on the adaptation of period interiors for wealthy clients in favor of community design projects including slum housing, a women's prison, and a Lower East Side youth center. Other interior design programs, such as the one at the Pratt Institute in Brooklyn, were similarly reoriented. While the outcome of the environmental design movement in architecture has been studied and subjected to critique, its influence on interior design pedagogy and practice has not. Using as a case study a program that experienced a radical version of this transformation, this essay will explore the moment in the mid-1960s when the criterion of taste was emphatically rejected. The introduction of environmental design principles into Parsons' curriculum did more than simply alter course content. In the name of greater social awareness and responsiveness, the new pedagogy blurred distinctions between disciplines and in the process toppled fundamental notions of design teaching and practice, including established means of representation and an orientation toward historical styles.

Fig. 1
A Place to Live exhibition,
Parsons School of Design,
April 1965

Conceptualized and guided by Howell, *A Place to Live* was a manifesto for a new vision of interior design. An iconoclast, Howell was probably disappointed that the show did not generate more public controversy. Reviews such as the one in *Interiors* were generally tolerant if not amused. Representatives of the newly formed Interior Design Educators Council (IDEC) toured the exhibition as part of their annual conference. Soon afterwards they issued their approved interior design curriculum, influenced in part by what they had seen.[2] Within the school, however, the battle lines were drawn. The new direction displayed in the show and the curriculum seemed drastic and wrong to many. In May 1966 a group of second-year students wrote a letter to the Alumni Association protesting the changes.

> Most of us came to Parsons...to pursue a course of concentrated study of High-style interiors....We understand that the Parsons Look is not necessarily a traditional look, that design covers all fields and can be studied in many ways, but we came to Parsons to learn how to produce that "special look"; that has been attained and maintained during this past half century.[3]

Although another, equally large, group of students wrote in support of Howell and the new curriculum, those who wrote in protest were concerned that the famed Parsons look was being abandoned. While the program quickly acquired a new version of the look during the 1970s, regret over the loss of the original, and speculation about what that look might resemble today, continues to reverberate.

Up until 1964 an education in interior design at Parsons meant an education in a very specific version of good taste. The original Parsons look was a hybrid of the turn-of-the-century New York style of decorating made popular by Elsie de Wolfe, mixed with the minimalist French luxury popularized by Jean-Michel Frank in the late 1920s. The look had its origins in the teaching of William Odom, known as "Mr. Taste," or "the inventor of smart, rich, high-style decorating," and his protégé Van Day Truex.[4] It was a luxury interior based on historical models, in particular an abstraction of the proportions, brightness, and relative emptiness of the eighteenth-century French townhouse, furnished with a few period-appropriate pieces along with some more contemporary items for contrast. Beyond the small world of the school, the look became a style vernacular that was widely exhibited in the design press and in popular media.

The look was transmitted with very little variation through the years, largely because of the limited number of people involved. Graduates became influential players in the small and elite New York interior design scene. They also became Parsons teachers, passing on what they had learned with only modest alteration.[5] Prominent alumni included Odom's pupil and informal business partner, Eleanor McMillen Brown. Through her own firm, McMillen Inc., she promoted the look almost exclusively, with occasional forays into art moderne and American colonial. She continued to exert a strong influence over the program and the profession in her role as a member of the board of trustees and employer of many Parsons graduates, including Albert Hadley.[6] The look was disseminated in new discipline-specific journals such as *Interior Design* and *Interiors* that had little use for the asceticism of high modernism. It became part of popular culture through its incorporation in department store windows and movie sets. For example, Parsons graduate William Pahlmann designed model rooms for the department store Lord and Taylor, while another graduate, Joseph B. Platt, became a Hollywood set designer and was responsible for blockbuster films including *Gone with the Wind* (1939) and *Rebecca* (1940). Together these Parsons alumni broadcast the look to a mass audience across the country and the world.

Until 1964 the interior design curriculum at Parsons was, as Henry-Russell Hitchcock described nineteenth-century architectural education, "a grounding in those styles considered most suitable for imitation."[7] Students studied for three years to gain a certificate in interior design.[8] The first year was dedicated to fundamentals of architecture and furniture design, form, color, composition, and decoration. In their second and third years, students concentrated on the study of historic styles. The vehicle was the measurement and representation of period rooms through richly rendered watercolor perspectives and technical drawings of details like moldings. **Fig. 2** As the school's 1949 catalog noted, "Of particular importance is the inculcation of the superior standards of taste for which Parsons School of Design has become distinguished."[9]

While the Parsons look was established and practiced in New York, its primary reference point was Paris, the center of American taste for nearly two centuries.[10]

Fig. 2 (top)
Three Parsons students making measured drawings of a side table, ca. 1940
Kellen Design Archives

Fig. 3 (bottom)
Three Parsons students making measured drawings in the Palazzo Ducale, Mantua, Italy, ca. 1925
Kellen Design Archives

Just as American architecture students went to the Beaux-Arts for training during the nineteenth century, after World War I Parsons interior design students went to Paris to be taught French style. In the early 1920s, Odom established an outpost at the Place des Vosges, where selected students spent a year of advanced study supplemented by a summer of sketching in Italy. **Fig. 3** In Paris they learned to translate French taste for the upper-middle-class design market in America. This was not the Paris of the avant-garde (which was in the process of shattering old standards of taste), or even the Paris of the 1925 Exposition Internationale des Arts Décoratifs et Industriels Modernes (where the luxury trade established its own modern aesthetic, dubbed art deco). The real draw was the long history of fine decorating on display in the homes of wealthy aristocrats.

Intellectually the Parsons pedagogy depended on ideas of *convenance* and *bienséance*, i.e., propriety and comfort, both defined according to standards of good taste established two centuries earlier by French masters including Jacques-François Blondel and Nicolas Le Camus de Mézières.[11] Technically the training was one of careful imitation and translation. Under faculty members Truex and Mildred Irby, Parsons students measured, drew, and learned to recombine the various elements of fashionable French interiors into new designs. **Figs. 4, 5** The chief medium was the interior perspective, rendered in watercolor and painstakingly constructed to depict the play and composition of colors, textures, and patterns on every surface. Students learned not only by making these detailed representations but also through osmosis. Commenting on his years living in Paris from 1925 to 1939, first as a student then as a faculty member, Truex said: "I walked in beauty." Late in his career, Truex summed up the school's philosophy in the following way: "basically our approach was always motivated and controlled by, let's give them as much as we can in the sense of eye, in the sense of quality and the sense of style."[12]

The interior design curriculum established at Parsons in the 1920s remained largely unchanged until the mid-1950s. By that time the Board of Trustees decided that the school was out of touch with the reality of design practice in postwar America. Wartime was a period of anonymous, bureaucratic design in the United States.[13] In its immediate aftermath, designers felt the pressure to build up the American economy through commercial and technological expertise. The discipline of interior design

Fig. 4 (top)
"Original design for a
small circular sitting room
combining features of various
18th century French styles
with modern features in
background," Parsons School
of Design catalog, 1927–28

Fig. 5 (bottom)
"Original Design—Library in
the Directoire Style," Parsons
School of Design catalog,
1933–34

expanded beyond its traditional focus on domestic interiors for elite private clients. In the world of business, the field of contract interiors created a broader basis for practice and demanded new design skills. Models of the modern middle-class house appeared on television and in magazines, introducing new styles and markets for home decoration. Finally, in education, the emergence of a new field of design practice, "environmental design," generated criteria against which to assess the performance of the interior.

Successive Parsons presidents Pierre Bedard, Sterling Callisen, and Francis Ruzicka attempted to align the school's curriculum more closely with contemporary social and economic concerns. In 1949 "low-budgeted housing" was introduced as an area of study within the interior design program.[14] In 1954 Bedard established a Department of Design in Industry (i.e., industrial design), and in 1957 he launched a short-lived Department of Design in Commerce, which offered classes in merchandising display and store design. By 1959 Parsons was rewriting its history, deliberately downplaying the idea of taste, along with importance of the Paris program and of its early administrators. Catalogs from this period explicitly described the all-encompassing importance of Parsons Paris as a strictly historical phenomenon. Though students could still study there, the administration emphasized the fact that New York was now the center of the school's activity.[15] President Ruzicka was the major agent of change. Citing long-standing complaints that the interior design department was moribund and the faculty intractable, Ruzicka was especially critical of what he called the "over-romanticization" of period study.[16] The most significant change began in 1964 when faculty members James Howell and Allen Tate, with the support of the administration, began to realign the curriculum with the new field of environmental design.

It is important to note that the reimagining of interior design education as a subset of the new field of environmental design did not follow but was contemporaneous with a similar reimagining of architecture. The concept of "environment" that emerged in North American universities in the 1950s enabled and encouraged a coordinated, systematic, and interdisciplinary approach to the fields of design and planning.[17] The environmental design movement, popularized by programs such as the one established at UC Berkeley in 1959, was based on an understanding of design as the total activity of arranging and building the world, deliberately disregarding the traditional distinctions between the disciplines of interior design, architecture, landscape architecture, and urban design.[18] In the writing of influential figures such as John McHale and Ian McHarg, the boundaries between "home" and "globe" were becoming less and less distinct or significant.[19]

The interdisciplinarity touted by advocates of environmental design was chiefly meant to integrate the fields of social and physical planning at all scales. The new approach was based on modernist ideas about the improvement of physical well-being for all and the betterment of social relations, an approach in which the concept of taste appeared to have no place. Tate equated an education in taste with elitism and a crass commercialism attuned to the upper-middle-class market for furniture and decoration—taste is that which sells, he said. On the occasion of Parsons' seventy-fifth anniversary in 1975, he summed up these changes: "In a world facing problems of ecology, over-population and all the attendant social ills, it is of a greater priority to learn how to create habitable spaces for the masses rather than drawing rooms for the few."[20] He encouraged students and faculty members to think of interior design as a method through which to challenge social convention, rather than reinforce it.

In the search for these "habitable spaces for the masses," the pedagogy of environmental design was characterized by three key objectives: a concentration on the process of design rather than the resulting form (i.e., on problem solving rather than form making); a focus on the creation of human environments rather than building technologies (i.e., on the space contained within the building and on the activities of its occupants rather than the makeup of the shell and its cladding); and finally, the rejection of the idea of designer-as-artist in favor of a community of diverse professionals whose members worked collectively, in much the same way that scientists did.[21]

Interior designers were more than happy to claim a stake in the expanded field of environmental design. The new discipline was conceived of as a collaborative effort on a huge scale, from the region and city to the individual room and pieces of furniture. In this context, interior design was an important component of a large and complex puzzle. The significance of the profession in the movement is evident in that the first issue of *Design and Environment* in 1970 featured an article titled "Interior Designers Discover Behavioral Research." It included a discussion of the Tektite II project by the U.S. Department of the Interior in collaboration with General Electric's Space Division, an underwater habitat designed for prolonged human occupation. In this way of thinking, interior design was not primarily confined to the private home, but an essential part of exciting new fields such as space and deep-sea exploration. **Fig. 6**

The movement toward environmental design that took place in interior design programs, notably at Parsons and Pratt, was partly promoted by the belief that architects were becoming more and more focused on large-scale urban problems, leaving the intimate space of the interior behind.[22] However, this intimate human environment was not the same one addressed by Elsie de Wolfe and William Odom. The environmental approach relied not on traditional ideas of taste but on investigation into physiology and the sciences of human behavior, especially psychology and sociology. Following the modernist paradigm, it aimed to better social relations by assuming absolute equality and by focusing efforts on the economically disadvantaged. The field was open for interior designers to reimagine their own particular skills in broad social and scientific terms.

In the philosophy of environmental design, the success of a particular project was assessed in relation to its performance rather than its appearance. Howell, who became chair of the department in 1965, redefined the discipline of interior design as "the shaping and conditioning of spaces into an optimum functional and psychological environment."[23] His philosophy is reflected in the 1965–66 curriculum. For many years the curriculum had centered on an eleven-credit second-year course in historic styles ("Period Color and Design"), taught by alumnus and successful society decorator Stanley Barrows. Under pressure from Ruzicka, Howell, and Tate, Barrows was encouraged to transform his course into a series of supporting lectures on the history of interior design, rather than the basis of knowledge for the whole program. Howell also introduced courses in material fabrication, as well as lighting and furniture design. The result was to remove the study of objects and fabrication methods away from the specific context of historical practice and instead to categorize them according to assumed objective and timeless principles. Finally the course "Drawing and Painting" was replaced by "Graphic Communications," rationalizing the process of representation. As in the field of architecture forty years earlier, watercolor perspectives representing the colors, textures, and patterns of interior surfaces lost their preeminence in favor of more scientific forms of representation—the plan, section, elevation, and most of all the axonometric—drawings that privileged abstract spatial relationships

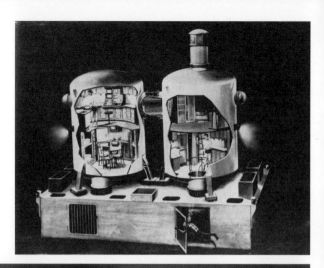

Fig. 6 (top)
Tektite II, 1970
U.S. Department of the Interior
and General Electric Space
Division

Fig. 7 (bottom)
Ms. Inez Croom, chair of the
Scholarship Committee of
the New York Chapter of
the American Institute of
Interior Designers, presents
the 1964 award to Mr. Joel
Mettler and Ms. Terri Mally,

both graduating students of
Parsons School of Design.
Kellen Design Archives

over tactile, material ones.[24] (For a time the approaches existed in tandem, which was confusing for the students. For example, a photograph of the work of two students taken in 1964 represents the two kinds of project coming out of the curriculum, one a traditional rendering of an interior perspective complete with decorative paneling and period furniture, the other a much more abstract rendering, one that, significantly, appears to have no walls.) **Fig. 7**

Besides altering the curriculum, Howell and Tate invited visiting faculty members from the natural and social sciences, including Paul A. Fine, a psychologist and sociologist, Albert Eide Parr, senior scientist at the American Museum of Natural History, and E. Lee Raney, a speech instructor at Columbia University. These changes predate Parsons' 1970 affiliation with the New School for Social Research, when it became possible for students to take classes in the humanities and social sciences as members of the larger institution.

As *Interiors* magazine noted in its review of the 1965 Parsons graduation show:

> What Parsons interior design students were doing, in effect, was assert-
> ing that their profession belongs in the forefront of the science of envi-
> ronmental psychology and urban sociology....Scientists, humanists,
> architects, and industrial designers are trying to build a body of scientific
> knowledge, based on painstaking research. But none of these professions
> has more practical contact with the interaction between environment
> and daily life than interior designers.[25]

For example, the Parsons 1966 end of year show featured a project for a prefabricated housing system made up of aluminum framing filled with modular panels, the type of project more often seen in architecture schools. The *Interiors* review stated, "It was as though student [John] Bray was calling attention to the fact that no one is better quali-
fied to design the objects which make up the immediate and human environment than the interior designer—and when this environment has to be mass-produced—well he can take care of that too."[26]

Though strongly resisted by many members of the existing faculty, these teaching methods were consistent with the ways in which some professional interior designers were reorienting their practices during the same time period, particularly those who focused on large-scale corporate interiors.[27] In 1967, former president of the National Society of Interior Designers C. James Hewlett founded the Interior Environments Research Council. This organization relied heavily on the work of anthropologist Edward T. Hall and his theory of "proxemics," the study of the culturally specific component of human concepts of space. As *Design and Environment* noted, the acceptance of these ideas within the design professions reflected "society's growing awareness that anthropology, psychology and human engineering provided, for the first time, a scientific foundation for measuring man's responses to interior settings."[28]

The core belief underlying environmental design, that spatial design has a direct and measurable impact on social behavior, led to a particular interest in the redesign of extreme social environments characterized by poverty and crime.[29] At Parsons, as at architecture schools during the same period, studio problems focused on socially worthy programs such as prisons, youth centers, and low-cost housing, all located far from the elegant drawing rooms of the Upper East Side. Between 1964 and 1969, Parsons studio projects included the redesign of Manhattan's notorious women's prison in Greenwich Village, as well as one on Riker's Island, and a youth center on the Lower East Side.[30] **Figs. 8, 9**

In working through these exercises, students were encouraged to focus not on the culturally constructed historical employment of styles, but on the supposedly objective science of psychology. One course, "Psychology of Perception," introduced students to the manipulation of light, color, and material in order to change the way people behave—ideas first explored at the Bauhaus. For example, the design for the Mobilization for Youth project included a series of colored directional baffles intended as wayfinding devices, and the women's prison featured "color bands in a spiral pattern to visually minimize long corridors; other corridors [were] visually shortened and widened by [the placement of] light fixture[s]...."[31] With this attention to the psychological and abstract aspect of color and form, interior design education at Parsons abandoned the particulars of period style that had defined the program since its inception sixty years earlier.

The mid-1960s reform of the Parsons program was a pivotal point in the history of both the institution and the discipline, one with lasting implications. In 1970

LIKE, MAN, IT'S FOR REAL

Seniors Rey, Kaplan, and Greene

Parsons seniors help Mobilization for Youth, Inc. brighten the future of its youthful clients. A class assignment that widened professional horizons, and that may stimulate actual remodeling, is illustrated with the design submitted by one of seven of the student teams.

Photos and Text by George McC. Whitney

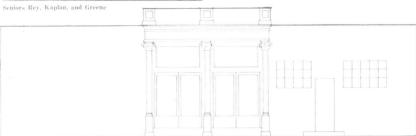

Below: Pre-Parsons Mobilization for Youth Job Center at 214 East Second Street.

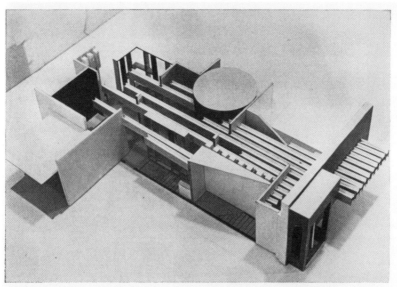

Three-dimensional scale model by Rey, Greene, and Kaplan, showing how structural lines of the marquee over windows at front of building are carried through full length of intake-reception area, serving to direct traffic as well as to house the vandal-proof lighting elements overhead.

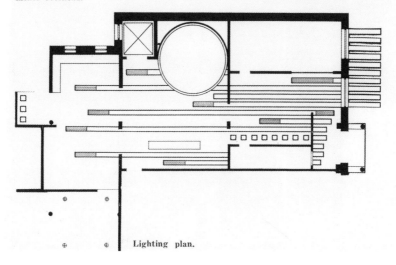

Lighting plan.

Figs. 8, 9

Luis Rey, Barbara Greene, and Howard Kaplan, interior design seniors at Parsons School of Design, proposal for Mobilization for Youth Job Center, East Second Street, New York City, May 1967

the department was renamed the Department of Environmental Design. Under Tate, who was named chairman in that same year, the faculty continued the pedagogical approach initiated five years earlier: attention to the psychological aspects of human behavior as motivators for design rather than historical precedents; choice of low-income community-based programs rather than those for elite clients; and emphasis on the connections between the different scales of design as component parts in the larger human environment. Over time the department also introduced attention to ecological issues in ways that anticipated our current concern with sustainability. **Fig. 10**

However, within some circles of the interior design world this moment is not remembered fondly. Some critics have charged that changes to the program and the abandonment of the Parsons look meant the loss of many positive attributes of the previous educational method, in particular: attention to the intimate character and scale of the interior surface; skill in specialist forms of fabrication and representation

Fig. 10
Students discussing a project
to construct tensegrities, 1972
Photograph courtesy of Casey
Coates Danson (Parsons 1975),
pictured third from right, smoking

(particularly training in material selection and watercolor rendering); and a thorough knowledge of the modes of taste that made up design history until the mid-twentieth century. These are valid criticisms. As Kent Kleinman points out elsewhere in this volume, it may be attention to the specificity of the surface and to the *sensus communis* of taste that gives interior design its particular claim on knowledge. But perhaps a synthesis of the two approaches is the most desirable outcome as we look forward. If the particular mode of knowing that characterizes early twentieth-century interior design practice (attention to surface, detail, and material, along with active engagement with the contemporary community of taste) could be synthesized with an updated "environmental approach" (one that is synchronized with other design disciplines and seriously addresses the problem of sustainability), then interior design might reclaim some aspects of its former territory in a productive rather than nostalgic way.

I am grateful to Wendy Scheir and the staff of the Anna-Maria and Stephen Kellen Archives Center at Parsons The New School for Design for their help in researching archival material.

1   "Parsons Exhibition; Seniors Scan Slum Housing," *Interiors* 124 (May 1965): 10.

2   Olga Gueft, "Education for Interiors at Parsons and Pratt," *Interiors* 125 (November 1965): 163.

3   Parsons School of Design Alumni Association. Events: Interior Design Department Student Protest and Counter-Protest, May 1966. Anna-Maria and Stephen Kellen Archives, Parsons The New School for Design.

4   "The Influence of William Odom on American Taste," *House and Garden* 90 (October 1946): 88, 93, 162. John Richardson, "The Sad Case of Mr. Taste," in *Sacred Monsters, Sacred Masters: Beaton, Capote, Dalí, Picasso, Freud, Warhol, and More* (New York: Random House, 2001), 64–71. On Truex, see "The Connoisseur: Late Dean of American Twentieth Century Design," *Antiques and Collectibles* 202 (1979): 232; Christopher Petkanas, "Van Day Truex: Master of Understatement," *House and Garden* 165, no. 1 (January 1993): 72–75, 119; Adam Lewis, *Van Day Truex: The Man Who Defined Twentieth-Century Taste and Style* (New York: Studio, 2001).

5   Stanley Barrows, "Recalling a Golden Era in Manhattan Design," *Architectural Digest* 46 (1989): 350–56.

6   On McMillen, see Erica Brown, *Sixty Years of Interior Design: The World of McMillen* (New York: Viking Press, 1982).

7   Henry-Russell Hitchcock, "Some Problems in the Interpretation of Modern Architecture," *JSAH* 2, no. 2 (April 1942): 29.

8   Beginning in 1945, Parsons also offered a four-year Bachelor of Science degree through an affiliation with New York University.

9   Parsons School of Design Catalog, 1949–50, 4. Anna-Maria and Stephen Kellen Archives, Parsons The New School for Design.

10   On the global importance of Parisian luxury goods, beginning in the eighteenth century, see Robert Fox and Anthony Turner, eds., *Luxury Trades and Consumerism in Ancien Régime Paris: Studies in the History of the Skilled Workforce* (Brookfield, VT: Ashgate, 1998), 99–137.

11   Nicolas Le Camus de Mézières, *The Genius of Architecture: Or the Analogy of that Art with our Sensations* (Santa Monica, CA: Getty Center for the History of Art and the Humanities, 1992); Robin Middleton, "Jacques-François Blondel and the Cours d'Architecture," *Journal of the Society of Architectural Historians of Great Britain* 18, no. 4 (1959); Richard A. Etlin, "'Les dedans,' Jacques-François Blondel and the System of the Home, c. 1740," *Gazette des Beaux-Arts* (April 1978): 137–47.

12   Van Day Truex, interview by Paul Cummings, November 15, 1971, Archives of American Art, Smithsonian Institution.

13   Andrew M. Shanken, *194X: Architecture, Planning, and Consumer Culture on the American Home Front* (Minneapolis, MN: University of Minnesota Press, 2009).

14   Parsons School of Design Catalog, 1949–50, 6.

15   Ibid.

16   President Francis Ruzicka, letter to Richard M. Paget, Chairman of the Board of Trustees, June 20, 1966, Anna-Maria and Stephen Kellen Archives, Parsons The New School for Design. The subject of this letter was "The Controversies Relating to the Interior Design Department."

17   Reinhold Martin, "Environment c. 1973," *Grey Room*, no. 14 (Winter 2004): 78–101.

18   The architecture program at the State University of New York, Buffalo, underwent a similar transformation under Michael Brill, with the help of Reyner Banham and John McHale.

19   John McHale, *The Ecological Context* (New York: George Braziller, 1970). See Alex Kitnick's essay in this volume for a closer look at the implications of McHale's writing for interior design.

20   "Evolution or Revolution? A Close Look at Parsons School of Design on its 75th Birthday," *Interior Design* 42 (May 1971): 86.

21   These aims were partly realized in the new professional associations spawned by the environmental design movement, including the Inter-Professional Council on Environmental Design, made up of members of the American Institute of Architects, the American Society of Engineers, the American Society of Landscape Architects, and the American Institute of Planners, founded in 1963, and new publications like the *Journal of Environmental Design*, founded 1965, and *Design and Environment*, founded in 1970.

22 Gueft, "Education for Interiors at Parsons and Pratt," 162. In 1965 Harold Elliot Leeds, chairman of the interior design department at Pratt, claimed that "the interior designer will gradually take over most of the responsibility for human environment at intimate scale."

23 James Howell, "The Interior Designer's Role Today," *Interior Design* 37 (July 1966): 115.

24 Yves-Alain Bois has discussed the ideological underpinnings of the modernist preference for the axonometric in his article, "Metamorphosis of Axonometry," *Daidalos*, no. 1 (1981): 41–58.

25 "Parsons Exhibition; Seniors Scan Slum Housing," *Interiors* 124 (May 1965): 10.

26 "Triumph at Parsons," *Interiors* 125 (July 1965): 12.

27 John Zeisel, "Interior Designers Discover Behavioral Research," *Design and Environment* 1, no. 1 (Spring 1970): 41–43. See also John Zeisel, "Behavioral Research and Environmental Design: A Marriage of Necessity," *Design and Environment* 1, no. 1 (Spring 1970): 50–51, 64–66, and John Zeisel, *Inquiry by Design: Tools for Environment-Behavior Research* (Cambridge: Cambridge University Press, 1984).

28 "Designers and Scientists Dedicated to Rebuilding the Environment," *Design and Environment* 1, no. 1 (Spring 1970): 19–25.

29 Daniel Barber has discussed the popularity of the prison as a studio problem in environmental design curricula in "Extreme Environmental Design: The 'Correctional Facilities' Studio at UC Berkeley College of Environmental Design, 1966–67," presented at the Studioscope Symposium, Harvard Graduate School of Design, April 13, 2007.

30 "Four Parsons Students Tackle Women's Prison Design," *Interiors* 127 (December 1967): 14; George M. Whitney, "Like, Man, It's for Real: Parsons Seniors Help Mobilization for Youth, Inc.," *Interiors* 126 (June 1967): 125; "The Environmental Approach; Senior Project of Parsons School of Design," *Interior Design* 39 (February 1968): 148–49, 168.

31 Ibid.

TECHNOLOGY IN/AND THE HOME

Alex Kitnick

In 1957 the artist, designer, and critic John McHale published an article about kitchen design in *Ark: The Journal of the Royal College of Art*, a periodical increasingly hip to the vicissitudes of popular culture.[1] Appearing alongside articles like "Dream Worlds, Assorted" and "Designing for Television," McHale's contribution is listed in the table of contents as "Technology in the Home," but at the top of the article itself a slightly modified title turns up, "Technology and the Home," framed in a large black rectangle of CinemaScope-like proportions.[2] The discrepancy in headings, though surely the result of editorial oversight, nevertheless suggests rather different relationships between the two key terms held up for discussion. Whereas the former phrasing proposes that technology finds its place *in* the home, in the latter technology *and* the home are placed next to one another like competing entities. In his essay, McHale followed this second line of interpretation, investigating some of the influences, challenges, and tensions that existed between the two terms at the time. Looking closely at the resistance of tradition and the force of innovation, McHale forecasted a vision of domestic life on the verge of radical change.

The kitchen was the best place to watch the sparring between technology and the home that was then playing out, McHale insisted, and he pointed to a number of commercial "packages" as offering particularly good vantage points for the match. The Frigidaire Kitchen of the Future, for example, contained seventeen distinct components within it, including a "roto-storage centre," "electro recipe file," "ultrasonic dishwasher," and "planning communications centre." **Fig. 1** By incorporating such technologies into a space where oven and stove had previously sufficed, the kitchen was shedding its identity as a place to prepare meals (the so-called "heart of the home"), and was instead turning into something more like a home office, a headquarters for domestic planning.[3] Despite these changes, McHale still found that even such up-to-date models were not fully forthcoming about the technologies of which they were made; they still looked like yesterday—indeed, like kitchens—with old-fashioned lines, discrete spaces, and fake wood surfaces kept intact. Interior design, in this instance, hadn't adapted to the lifestyle changes of its inhabitants, or the technologies they used. It simply provided an armature for a constellation of appliances, trying to contain them without really listening to their implications.

As an example of a project that attempted to register the full force of technology, McHale pointed to the House of the Future designed by the architects Alison and

Fig. 1 (top)
Frigidaire Kitchen of the
Future, 1957

Fig. 2 (bottom)
Alison and Peter Smithson,
House of the Future, *Daily
Mail* Ideal Home exhibition,
1956. The mobile kitchen cart
can be seen on the left.

Peter Smithson for the 1956 *Daily Mail* Ideal Home exhibition.[4] **Fig. 2** As in the Frigidaire unit, high-tech gadgets also appeared here, but in this instance they were incorporated differently, with many of the kitchen's traditional functions relegated to a mobile cart. The house's seemingly vacuum-formed shape, moreover, made it look like an appliance itself while simultaneously imparting a sense of corporeality to the structure, bending to the curves of its inhabitants as it did. To borrow a phrase from the media theorist Marshall McLuhan, the House of the Future transformed housing technology into an "extension of man" by reconfiguring its traditional form; it placed such an emphasis on interiority, for example, that it more or less bypassed any need for an exterior. Meant to function as one cellular unit abutting others in an infinitely expandable grid—a structure that stood both alone and together at once—the House of the Future was almost a cocoon. With its facade stripped away, it served as a diorama into which visitors to the exhibition could peer, providing an image of a life to come. Inside, McHale insisted, was an example of how mechanization might fundamentally affect established patterns of living. Here, technology plus home added up to a genuinely new thing.

The increasing prominence of technology in the domestic sphere in the post-war years, of course, had not happened overnight. McHale noted an important precedent, as well as a still unheeded call for change, in the work of the visionary inventor R. Buckminster Fuller, whose never-realized Dymaxion House of 1927 not only incorporated technology within it but was also a piece of technology itself—an item of mass production.[5] Like a car or airplane, the Dymaxion House was fabricated out of mass-produced parts—pneumatic partitions, sponge floors, and climate-controlled spaces. "The Dymaxion House was never intended as a design for a unique, one-of-a-kind building," McHale noted in a book on the inventor. "Its true function was to be the prototype for a world-wide housing industry, similar in scope to the auto, shipbuilding, or airplane industries but different in that it would rent its products on a service, repair, and new model replacement basis rather like a telephone company."[6] Fuller's house, in other words, was not much like a traditional house at all. Never trained as an architect, Fuller was able to free himself from the conventions of style, form, and taste that bound the discipline of architecture together. He was primarily concerned with the "performance" of the building and its interior, which, for him, extended to the altruistic goal of trying to house as many people as possible.

In looking at Fuller's models, one can see that performance was the point. From an aesthetic angle, the Dymaxion House did not shy away from its engagement with industry, even if this was simply a by-product of its means of manufacture. "The first version of the Dymaxion House was envisaged as hexagonal in shape," McHale noted, "and hung from a central mast, to be air-conditioned, with built-in furnishing, a packaged kitchen and automatic laundry equipment."[7] Contrary to the traditional idea of the house, built to last out of bricks and stone, the Dymaxion was a metal machine, meant to be used for a finite period of time and then tossed out. In many ways, it was a product for a new generation at home on the road, "an autonomous, self-maintaining unit suitable, in a period of mobility and transience, to erect anywhere, and be close to an expendable structure like the automobile."[8] **Fig. 3** Despite this, McHale's primary disappointment with Fuller was that his designs were not like automobiles enough. Or, to put it differently, they were more like Model Ts. Though Fuller's work used the techniques and technologies of the automotive industry, it nevertheless refused to incorporate its symbolic vocabularies like the Smithsons' House of the Future did. Fuller's designs were industrial products, and they looked the part. They were not gussied up with aesthetic components to entice consumers and spark trends. No styling was applied to them.

For Fuller, this denigration of aesthetics had its reasons. He often chided the first generation of modern architects, such as Le Corbusier, for calling themselves functionalists when he considered them to be more interested in the aesthetics of function—the look of grain silos and the lines of cruise ships—than in function itself.[9] His work was to be an antidote to that. If McHale agreed with Fuller's critique of Le Corbusier, however, he saw his refusal to engage questions of symbolism and style as a missed opportunity. McHale believed that one had to work within a given situation. If Fuller's designs were to catch on, McHale reasoned, they would have to appeal to a public accustomed to the allure of images and advertisements, and would therefore need to be styled accordingly. It was not that Fuller's inventions should engage the aesthetics of function but rather they should attach themselves to the look of the future.

As they were, Fuller's structures, in many ways, might be thought of as off-road vehicles. His frequent description of his "living units" as autonomous and self-sustaining invokes certain ideas of independence and freedom—a kind of better living through

Fig. 3
R. Buckminster Fuller,
Dymaxion Dwelling Machine,
ca. 1944
Courtesy, The Estate of
R. Buckminster Fuller

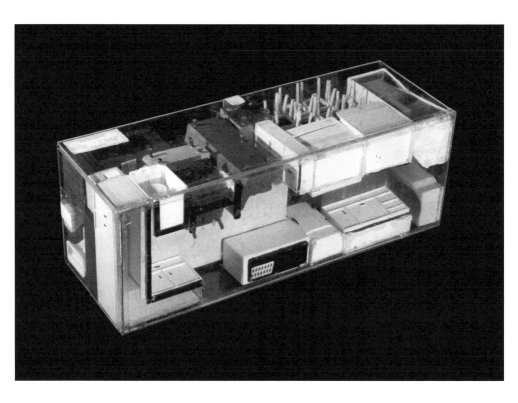

Fig. 4
R. Buckminster Fuller,
Autonomous Living Package,
1948–49
Courtesy, The Estate of
R. Buckminster Fuller

technology—closely associated with the rhetoric of the American automobile, and yet at the same time, his language is also closely related to a feeling of anxiety and fear. The Cold War hovers above many of his designs, delivering a sense of what it might be like to go it alone. His "Autonomous Living Package" of 1948–49, for example, was designed according to his "Universal Requirements Check List," which, as its name suggests, details "an exhaustive planning list of design needs in the human living pattern, real and to be anticipated, from those of simple survival during natural cataclysm, to the need for 'conning' the environment through communications—movies, TV, radio, books, etc."[10] **Fig. 4** Something of this desire for self-containment is visible in the Smithsons' project as well, with its encapsulated courtyard and tube of "unbreathed air."

The irony of such claims for autonomy, however, becomes apparent when looking at the networks these structures require. Indeed, these projects are organisms that need to be constantly replenished, fed with air, and "conned" with communications. Frigidaire, Fuller, and the House of the Future all brought technologies *into* the home, connected it to an outside world, and hooked it up to a wider network. Just as this was happening, however, the home was also expanding outward, giving rise, as McHale put it, to a number of "home extensions—like the auto, the Espresso café, the Wimpey bar, the movies—and even the pub," thereby taking typically private pastimes into the public realm.[11] A double movement took root here: just as the home brought the outside in, it also dispersed into a wide variety of forms. On the one hand, this allowed for a kind of "global interior"—a site where one can view endless flows of images and information—while on the other, it led the way to the domestication of space that we see around us everywhere today, from the simulated living rooms of Barnes & Noble and Starbucks to the increasingly chic quarters of hospitals.[12] It was not only the home that was transformed, in other words, but public space as well.

Over the course of his career, McHale theorized the idea of home extensions on an increasingly vast scale until he saw the world itself as a kind of home. (Notions of public and private were more or less tossed out the window.) In his 1970 book *The Ecological Context*, McHale points out that ecology, the scientific study of the relationship between organisms and their environment, literally means "house-knowledge."[13] "From the roots of 'house-knowledge,'" he continues, "we can assume a definition of applied human ecology as 'planetary housekeeping.'" By this time, McHale was possibly more interested in inventorying and managing the Earth's resources than he was in domestic space, and yet the term "home" still resonates here as more than a metaphor.[14] If the globe is an expanded house, the house is also a localized globe, and this has perhaps never been truer than it is today. If the contemporary house incorporates a wide range of technologies within it, and is therefore already connected to the outside world, we might ask if one might be able to do "planetary housekeeping" from the house itself or if one is relegated to a position of passive spectatorship? Such a question would seem to have important repercussions for the discipline of interior design, linking it up, once again, to an expanded practice of environmental design.

In his 1969 book *The Architecture of the Well-Tempered Environment*, architectural historian Reyner Banham, an old colleague of McHale's from London's Independent Group, offered a history of the role of technology in architecture, chronicling advances from ventilation and air conditioning to inflatable structures and fluorescent lighting, which not only led up to the present, but also projected into the future by offering a dose of criticism to the discipline of architecture. In addition to documenting the pitfalls of the past, such as the refusal of modern architects to properly engage technology (a critique not so different from Fuller's), Banham chastised contemporary architects for not paying sufficient attention to the primacy of technology in their own work.[15] In Banham's eyes, many architects were still overly concerned with questions of style and form when problems of environment were of the utmost importance.[16] This schism, he wrote, had come about as the result of mechanization. Given the increasing and inevitable primacy of technology in the home, the inside of the house had more or less been allowed to cleave from the outside, the exterior or facade seemingly becoming an autonomous entity from the space within.[17] Architects subsequently took this division as a given; instead of integrating the two (inside and out, technology and building), or ceding their attention to mechanical services, they focused primarily on the exterior, attending to formal values such as style, volume, space, and decoration. As a result, the interior was literally walled off. Banham's book was meant as a kind of counter-history to such a trend, showing new ways in which technology and architecture might be thought of holistically, and how the interior might be thought of in relation to the larger environment in which it existed.

Today, Banham's words still ring true, but in addition to mechanical services, a much wider range of concerns has to be taken into account when thinking about a building's environment. The glut of information, images, and technologies currently available has expanded infinitely—a fact that many architects, interior designers, and clients still fail to deal with adequately. To take a rather pedestrian example, the *New York Times* recently published an article, "How Smart Could I Make My Dumb Manhattan Apartment?" The piece profiled CytexOne, a company that claims to connect an audio-video system to an "environment" (CytexOne's word), which consists of lighting, heating, motorized blinds, and a security system starting for $25,000.[18] (The mention here of a security system might also remind us of the "fear situation" we live in, one not so different perhaps from the Cold War situation that McHale and Fuller found themselves enmeshed in. Indeed, for every claim of openness and free exchange today, we see another border and checkpoint go up.) The CytexOne system is something like the gadgetry of the Frigidaire unit that we first looked at, and similar questions again seem appropriate. Does this hyper-fetishistic attention to services truly do justice to the ways in which patterns of life are changing?

These are the very questions facing the discipline of interior design today. New technologies cannot simply be borrowed and imported; the designer must find proper and convincing forms to forge a well-tempered environment. In many cases, it seems that this will consist of opening up the interior to an outside world in new and challenging ways so as to trouble regimes of passivity and isolation. In searching for such solutions, one should remember McHale's suggestion to Fuller that one attend to one's working context in all its nuances. This does not mean that the market should be pandered to, but rather, as the Smithsons understood, that the most utopian forms are the ones that immerse themselves most deeply in the possibilities of their own moment.

1   For more on *Ark*, see Alex Seago, *Burning the Box of Beautiful Things: The Development of a Postmodern Sensibility* (Oxford: Oxford University Press, 1995).

2   John McHale, "Technology and the Home," *Ark: The Journal of the Royal College of Art*, no. 19 (1957): 24–27.

3   Tomás Maldonado, *Design, Nature, and Revolution: Toward a Critical Ecology* (New York: Harper & Row, 1972), 48. Indeed, the home office would soon become a reality. In 1972,

Maldonado wrote the "systems engineers" were "splitting up office work into as many parts as there are employees' homes. Thus, the home of the employee would be transformed into a 'domicile office,' into a small work unit perfectly equipped with technical means of communication, calculation, and programming, so that the employee could do all his office tasks at home. He would be able to do any kind of work that requires the elaboration and management of information: receiving, listing, verifying, evaluating, deciphering, interpreting, storing, and producing and transmitting messages." The result of all this, he insisted, would be "desocialization."

4   For a nuanced reading of the House of the Future in these terms, see Beatriz Colomina, "Unbreathed Air 1956," *Grey Room*, no. 15 (Spring 2004): 28–59.

5   Dymaxion was a neologism made from the words "dynamism," "maximum," and "ion." For an interesting take on Fuller's domestic projects, see Federico Neder, *Fuller Houses: R. Buckminster Fuller's Dymaxion Dwellings and Other Domestic Adventures* (Baden, Switzerland: Lars Müller, 2008).

6   John McHale, *R. Buckminster Fuller* (New York: George Braziller, 1962), 18.

7   McHale, "Technology and the Home," 24.

8   Ibid.

9   McHale, *R. Buckminster Fuller*, 19. "Fuller's criticism of the International Style as a 'fashion inoculation,' though harsh, is quite justified, for he sees that it was overconcerned with the *visual* aspect of both buildings and machine products, while structural function and capability had passed over into the *invisible* terms of hidden alloy strengths and instrumental tolerances."

10   Buckminster Fuller, "Universal Requirements Check List," *Architectural Design* 30, no. 3 (March 1960): 101–10. McHale wrote a preface to Fuller's text.

11   Marshall McLuhan, *Understanding Media: Extensions of Man* (New York: McGraw-Hill, 1964), 19. Fuller noted this early on, conceiving of the car as an extension of the house. See, for example, his Dymaxion car of 1933, which was simultaneously both a piece and satellite of his Dymaxion House. The idea of extensions was also central to the work of a number of other thinkers in the 1950s and 60s, and especially to McLuhan, who dubbed all media "extensions of man." "If clothing is an extension of our private skins to store and channel our own heat and energy," McLuhan wrote in *Understanding Media: Extensions of Man*, "housing is a collective means of achieving the same end for the family or the group." In positing "housing" as the rubric with which "heat" and "energy" are controlled, McLuhan imagined the domestic not only as a primarily technical matter but also as a malleable thing that could take a number of different forms.

12   I thank Susan Yelavich for helping me draw out these points.

13   John McHale, *The Ecological Context* (New York: George Braziller, 1970), 1. Mark Wigley also calls attention to this passage in his essay "Recycling Recycling," in *Eco-Tech: Architecture of the In-Between*, ed. Amerigo Marras (New York: Princeton Architectural Press, 1999), 39–49.

14   This said, McHale was still deeply invested in the idea of housing on a global scale. For more on this, see John McHale, "World Dwelling," *Perspecta: The Yale Architectural Journal* 11 (1967): 120–29.

15   This was at least partially the fault, Banham stressed, of the first generation of architectural historians that chronicled modern architecture by focusing more on form than environmental technology.

16   Indeed, such a schism would become exacerbated with the full flowering of postmodern architecture just a few years later.

17   Reyner Banham, *The Architecture of the Well-Tempered Environment*, 2nd ed. (Chicago: University of Chicago Press, 1984), 95–100.

18   Joyce Wadler, "How Smart Could I Make My Dumb Manhattan Apartment?" *New York Times*, March 17, 2010.

Interview with Stephen and Timothy Quay: To Those Who Desire Without End

Born near Philadelphia, Stephen and Timothy Quay relocated to London in the mid-1960s and have achieved an international reputation as among the most original voices in animation filmmaking. The 1984 *The Cabinet of Jan Svankmajer*, dedicated to the Czech animation master, the eleven-minute *This Unnameable Little Broom* of 1985, based on the *Epic of Gilgamesh*, and the twenty-one-minute *Street of Crocodiles* of 1986, based on the 1934 novel by Polish author Bruno Schulz, brought the Quay brothers early and wide acclaim as chroniclers of the characters and environs of a dystopic, mid-twentieth-century *Mitteleuropa*. Film critic Michael Atkinson has aptly called their works "sleep-walks through environments crushed by the torque of industrial progress." In addition to the animation films, the Quay corpus includes feature films, opera and performance sets, and "projection" projects throughout Europe. In 2010, the twins spoke with Kent Kleinman in Ithaca on the occasion of an exhibition of their film decors, and in the London studio where the Quays have worked for almost three decades.

Kent Kleinman: You've decided to allow your film sets to be exhibited as stand-alone models. When you're making these decors, do you conceive of them as comprehensive environments or do you always imagine them as fragments to be manipulated in the film editing process?

> **QUAY:** When we were first asked to exhibit the decors we were very suspicious and fearful if they would be able to hold their fiction. Their rightful place is within the cinematic experience. They're really for the camera to traverse, for light and music and narrative to pass over and through them. They are instruments, not objects. But we think it's very important that the sets announce a quality to launch the imagination.

KK: The cinematic eye is different from the roving eye of an exhibition viewer, the eye of an occupant in space. If the eye is analogous to the camera, the sets and the films of the sets are very different entities.

QUAY: Yes, that's true. For us the power is how we direct you with our eye, and we direct your eye with the all-seeing eye of the camera. When you put your eye to the eyepiece, it's a scared space. It's a final space too, like a beautiful coffin.

KK: But your sets are unlike stage sets or even traditional movie sets. Theater sets, at least those designed for proscenium contexts, have privileged aspects, governed by rules of sight and an economy of exposure. Traditional movie sets are art-directed only for the precise and predetermined zone of relevance set by the camera's lens. But your decors seem to have no obvious filmic boundary. They are congested like lived tableaus, which invites a certain undisciplined viewing into places where the camera may never look.

QUAY: On their own the decors are just holding their breath, just sitting there, open to the eye. You can actually read the space, you can step back and appreciate it. In cinema you don't have the time to read or investigate the space because you're being absorbed by the flow of the narrative.

KK: Well, you ordain the cut, you get to determine how long you look at something.

QUAY: Yes—"Here, have a glimpse!" That's the maximum of control factor.

KK: Yet when you're making these models, you do not seem to be governed by their cinematic relevance only.

QUAY: No, they are full...

QUAY: ...and self-sufficient.

KK: You painted the backsides, you treated the undersides, there is no obvious backstage. Instead there's a rabid thoroughness with these models, as if you were anticipating that they would be discovered in the unscripted way with which actual interiors are experienced.

> **QUAY:** When we're cruel to ourselves, one of our criticisms is to say that we lost the fiction, we didn't give the right density. The density of the fiction is really crucial *and* it's in proportion to the density of the actual fabricating of the decors themselves. The decors must smuggle the content of the fiction, if they don't you've lost immediately. Sometimes when we finish at night, we might accidentally have put a random lens, like a huge telephoto, on the camera. When we come back in the morning we say to ourselves, I think we're starting with a long shot where you see the entire decor, but then we put our eye to the eyepiece and suddenly realize that you're in a fantastic close-up. And you say: "That's where we should be starting!" So the craftsmanship has to hold up to this kind of accidental discovery.

KK: You start with a puppet armature that is completely mechanical, right?

> **QUAY:** Mechanical! You start with a naked ball and socket armature.

> **QUAY:** And then we clad it with balsa wood.

> **QUAY:** And then dress it with fabric. But the joints have to stay clean. You have to have a slit in the fabric in case you want to go in with a screwdriver to tighten up the joints.

(overleaf)
Decor
Street of Crocodiles, 1986

QUAY: Surgical opportunities.

QUAY: But you really build for the face.

QUAY: You have to sculpt the face. But the eyes are utterly crucial. All our puppets suffer from scopophilia. They're haunted by vision and search incessantly.

QUAY: You use real glass eyes, because they reflect light. It's very important that the puppets have light in their eyes, like in *Street of Crocodiles*, where the eyes have this glow. Bruno Schulz wrote about this milky light falling from above as though through glass roofs...

QUAY: "Dead light," he called it.

**Principal puppet cladding
detail
Street of Crocodiles, 1986**

QUAY: Usually we start with the decors but for *Crocodiles*, the first thing that was built was the main puppet. That struck the tone. He was a sort of stalker and an outsider figure. He wandered through this Schulzian zone completely fascinated. He was searching for epiphanies and for the chance encounter. You just needed a character who was tall and gaunt and obsessed. But then you say, "What is the fiction of his surroundings?" With Schulz, in particular, it was a realm of what he called degraded reality. Every space was in massive decay but it was as though he was searching for the inside lining of things. He saw the marvelous in the poetic ascension of everyday matter.

KK: You pick the fabrics and make the costumes for the puppets. In some cases you used almost the same fabrics on the puppets as on

Decor detail
Street of Crocodiles, 1986

(overleaf)
Tailor's shop decor
Street of Crocodiles, 1986

the wall of the interior spaces. In the set for *Rehearsals for Extinct Anatomies* you actually used an entire black-and-white-striped shirt to clad the walls; the buttons and buttonholes are clearly legible.

> **QUAY:** In *Rehearsals* we started with the decor. *Rehearsals* was shot in black and white, so we actually chose only black and white material. We could have chosen colored material, but you know it's in black and white, so everything was reduced to black and white, the character's dress, the floor pattern, even the fabric on the bed.

KK: And the fabric on the walls, which is of course at a 1:1 scale.

> **QUAY:** Precisely, precisely.

Tailor's shop decor detail
Street of Crocodiles, 1986

(top)
Gilgamesh and Enkidu
puppets
*This Unnameable Little
Broom*, 1985

(bottom)
Decor detail
*Rehearsals for Extinct
Anatomies*, 1987

(overleaf)
Decor
*Rehearsals for Extinct
Anatomies*, 1987

KK: The distinction between building an interior and constructing a character blurs in your work. Both are Arcimboldo-like assemblages of disparate objects of divergent scales that merge into apparent coherence. The puppet representing the famed Czech animation filmmaker Jan Svankmajer, for example, is a collage of found objects. Decrepit compass dividers are Svankmajer's arms, a dated Czech postage stamp is Svankmajer's face. And a large Arcimboldo print decorates the wall behind the Svankmajer figure in the opening scene, like an ancestral portrait, looking down on his progeny.

QUAY: Svankmajer wouldn't let us interview him. And we had this stamp from our father's stamp album. It's from 1930, so it would have been in circulation around the time that Svankmajer was born. And we suddenly realized that with the close-up lens, that in this

(previous spread)
Black room decor
*The Cabinet of Jan
Svankmajer*, 1984

Svankmajer puppet detail
*The Cabinet of Jan
Svankmajer*, 1984

stamp there's both the representation of Svankmajer as the alchemist of Prague, and the "Castle" of Rudolf II. So it was the linchpin. And again, it was that real size of a genuine postage stamp that became the catalyst to generate the entire film.

KK: Did that set the scale?

> **QUAY:** That set the scale, the entire scale. The proportions had to develop from that. And then we built three decors: the white room, the gray room, and the black room. The black room was where he worked with the child. The gray room was where he had all the drawers where he kept his archives. And the white room was the child's room, the metaphysical playroom with lessons in tactile apprehension.

KK: So the stamp was the origin.

> **QUAY:** Precisely.

KK: That detail sets the scale of the figure. The figure sets the scale of the worktable, which set the scale...

> **QUAY:** The scale of the walls.

> **QUAY:** That's it exactly. So where most people would start probably with a drawing, we start literally, physically, with an object. We can draw but some things, particularly objects, force you to work immediately in the third dimension. We'll make very rough sketches but...

> **QUAY:** ...everything is mere conjecture until we actually start building. What we like to do best is just start physically with the material, whether it's the puppet or the set. There's always the initial hunt

both for specific objects, the details, and the landscape that will set off these objects. Everything is a process of discovery.

KK: This fluidity seems to transfer into the very nature of your enclosures. Most of your spaces are interiors, apparently bounded by floors and walls and corners. When I see a floor represented, I typically understand the floor to be the thing that separates stories; I can count on it. I can walk across it. It will hold my weight. It's an inert datum. I understand walls to contain, to be impervious except to particular openings, like windows or doors, and the doors can either be open or closed. The space is a determined volume and activity happens inside it. But in your work it seems like the fixed vessel is so much of a protagonist that none of these conventions can be assumed. In *Rehearsals*, the very stripes of the wallpaper seem to vibrate. There's a quality of fixity to physical space that you are bent on upending.

QUAY: In *Rehearsals*, we put very thin wire just slightly in front of the wallpaper and plucked them so you get the feeling that the wall and the stripes of the wallpaper aren't stable. The space has to be in flux. Our characters always tend to enter into a space that's powerfully in flux or is concealing its potential; they tend to be baffled by the space, it's full of traps, holes that, if an errant subject comes into the frame, can clamp down at the click of a finger. Somebody can come along and energize a space and suddenly a wall's released, a drawer flies open! We're always thinking that the space that we set up is initially sort of a false front, which is going to reveal, little by little…

QUAY: …that it has a desire, some secret desire…

QUAY: …and that the space itself also dreams or that it wants to exert its presence and say, "I too am made up of the following, and

I'm not inert, but I'm constantly in flux and I will perpetrate certain things, whether you like it or not." We like spaces that have a very charged and concealed atmosphere.

KK: It sounds like the space almost has agency: it has desire, mood, it can assert itself and open itself up, the kind of properties you would normally associate with a subject.

QUAY: Yes, we put all that into the decor. I think that initially this came about because we were terribly frightened when we did our first puppet film, *Nocturna Artificialia.* We had a puppet that didn't have a proper armature—it was one of those armatures you can buy in an art shop. It was so uncontrollable that we started thinking: let's put the whole world around him into a massive flux to compensate for its inactivity. It's sort of what Jack Cole did when he choreographed for Marilyn Monroe. Because he knew that she couldn't dance, he made sure everything around her moved so as to give the impression that she was just alive with fire!

KK: So would it be fair to say that the decor can assume the same status as the characters in terms of narrative potential?

QUAY: Absolutely. The space is the poetic vessel that holds the drama, but it also shapes it. It is a powerful force that the viewer has to contend with. And certain objects ferment your desire, they're restless, they're never dead.

KK: In your decors, the accumulation of artifacts makes it almost impossible to know where the actual enclosure or the structure is. Objects accumulate to the point where "decoration" takes over the principal architectural work of enclosure. This is even more extreme in the actual interior of your studio.

QUAY: We don't go around with a bag on our shoulders, but we're always collecting intuitively. We are constantly searching. You'll see something and you'll grab it and you'll put in on a shelf or next to some other object. And then three weeks later or four months later you'll say, ah! there's a collision there, a secret alloy that we hadn't foreseen.

KK: It's impossible not to think of Walter Benjamin when thinking of collecting and the interior. Benjamin offered several tropes for the pursuit of knowledge, one being the collector. But another is the *Lumpensammler*, which is a special case of the collector. The rag-picker has no use for large, meta-narratives with grand historical sweeps. Instead, he picks up scraps, in Benjamin's specific example scraps of discarded language, words like "humanity" and "compassion," but

Quay studio interior,
London, 2010
Courtesy, Stephen and
Timothy Quay

they could be scraps of images, objects, sounds. I think of you as *Lumpensammlers*. The wallpaper you used in *This Unnameable Little Broom*—you said that you recovered it, all stained, from the trash outside of Freud's Bergstrasse apartment. The anonymous double-hung window in *In Absentia* that you salvaged, not to mention the dozens of anonymous rusty thimbles and screws you rescued from oblivion and featured so prominently in *Crocodiles*. Even dust and grime are conserved in your work from the cleansing deluge of modernity. I think of you as the *Lumpensammlers* of stains and patinas.

> **QUAY:** This is the side of Benjamin to which we really subscribe. Things are discarded because people think they have no further life. Nobody expects anything to happen with anonymous objects. But stains record history. The texture of rust holds history.

> **QUAY:** We've always been fascinated by anonymous architecture, and *Crocodiles* was entirely based on our documenting Krakow, Warsaw, and specifically the Praga district of Warsaw. We saw window displays in there of such bold poverty, a few items: six shoe cleats arranged in a graceful arc. The shop owner simply said, "I'm just going to make a modest arrangement." And they were gorgeous. This was in the late '70s under difficult times but somehow the shop fronts were richer for all their clear poverty. In terms of our approach to the realms of puppets and decors and animation, Robert Walser wrote something very beautiful. He says that there is everyday life and there is dream life, but for him there is also a *Zwischenwelt*—an "in-between-world"—and it was something his writings did achieve and it's something that we've always aimed for in our own work.

> There's a part of our work where we're very active, when we're perpetrating events. But at other points there's passivity, where we're just alert, deciding between forcing things and just letting things…

> **QUAY:** …unhappen.

Portfolio:
James Casebere

Lois Weinthal

James Casebere's models—extraordinary fabrications of haunting interiors made with such finely observed details, such precisely rendered finishes, and such convincingly conjured atmospherics that they seem to be the products not of artifice and stagecraft but of time and space—are contrivances, the means and not the end of the work.

For his process, the artist documents actual environments, sometimes institutional fragments of cells and corridors, occasionally abstract enclosures (*Tunnel #2*, 2003), infrequently historically specific sites (*Mosque (after Sinan) #3*, 2007), and not infrequently familiar domestic interiors (*Green Staircase #1*, 2001). The tools used to extract information from these existing settings are customary to practitioners of the building arts: plans, sections, dimensioned drawings of key details, and as-built photographs.

The "as-built" is transferred into the studio for translation to scaled model. But here Casebere's methodology diverges from mere transcription and is in fact far removed from that of traditional representation—the goal is not faithfulness. Each construction involves addition, subtraction, and reconfiguration. The models are not abstractions; far too much detail is retained or, in the case of the decay and catastrophe, added. They are studiously imperfect analogs, clearly associated with, and just as clearly independent from, the condition of the original site. The models are essentially doubles.

Doubling is not reproduction or replication; it operates in the opposite direction, as division, as a splitting of self from self. Doubling is a strange twinning that does not yield more but less, signaling and producing a crisis of identity—that which was once complete, known, and stable is now partial, haunting, and volatile. In the domain of literature, Freudian psychologist Otto Rank traced the remarkable reversibility of the concept, from embodiment of man's immortal soul to herald of man's inevitable death.[1] Reflections in watery surfaces feature prominently in writings of the double, as mysterious resemblances that detach themselves from and haunt their referents, presaging confrontation and collapse. The double serves as a prophecy, a specter that worms its way through our psychic systems of order and denial. Is there a spatial, environmental equivalent? In his etymological search for the linguistic origins of the uncanny, Freud unearthed a term that he never developed but that deserves a place in the lexicon of the spatial uncanny, and serves well to describe Casebere's interiors: *locus suspectus*.[2]

Casebere's constructions do not hide their artificiality, their shadowy materiality, their unnaturalness and insubstantiality. The tabletop constructs are, in fact, only stage sets, scaffoldings of foamcore, resin, gesso, and paint, held together with hot-glue and drafting tape. Like some laboratory apparatus, the models are armatures for controlled experiments in material and light. For Casebere does not only form space, he also shapes light and air that acquire an almost physical presence. In *Green Staircase #1*, for example, Casebere precisely directs light to project onto the staircase from the second level implying windows above, yet light enters the interior from another direction, skimming and reflecting off the flooded floor. Rays bounce off the lower portion of the walls and floors as if the entire space were a study in optics.

Optics and light are in fact at the very core of Casebere's work, for only the photographs (not the models) are displayed publicly. The photographs are presented in a very specific way that heightens their affective power. Often, he does not frame his prints but sandwiches them between sheets of Plexiglas and displaces them slightly off the wall so they appear to float. Also, the photographs are large: *Green Staircase #1*, measuring six feet high by four feet wide, is a typical format, and is scaled to approach the size of the built world.

Thus we are compelled to acknowledge the audacity of Casebere's project, for, as every architectural renderer knows, miniaturization disguises manual imperfection. Massively enlarged, the model assumes an illicit presence, flaunting its artifice almost at the scale of the actual environment. Enveloping the viewer, these images become both materially and psychically transferable back to the world of brute construction, mirroring our condition, and staging the final and fatal confrontation of self to self.

James Casebere is the recipient of numerous fellowships including the National Endowment for the Arts, the New York Foundation for the Arts, and the John Simon Guggenheim Memorial Foundation. His work has been collected by museums worldwide, including the Museum of Modern Art, the Whitney Museum of American Art, the Solomon R. Guggenheim Museum, the Jewish Museum, the Metropolitan Museum of Art, the Walker Art Center, the Museum of Contemporary Art in Los Angeles, the Los Angeles County Museum of Art, and the Victoria and Albert Museum in London. Casebere lives and works in New York.

1   Otto Rank, *The Double: A Psychoanalytical Study*, trans. Harry Tucker Jr. (1925; London: Maresfield Library, 1989).

2   Sigmund Freud, "The Uncanny," in *The Uncanny* (London: Penguin Books, 2003), 125.

<u>Green Staircase #1</u>, 2001
Digital chromogenic print

<u>Yellow Hallway #2</u>, 2001
Digital chromogenic print

<u>Spanish Bath (horizontal)</u>, 2003
Digital chromogenic print

La Alberca, 2005
Digital chromogenic print

Maghreb, 2005
Digital chromogenic print

<u>Abadia from Lower Left</u>, 2005
Digital chromogenic print

<u>Flooded Street</u>, 2008
Digital chromogenic print

<u>Spiral Staircase</u>, 2003
Digital chromogenic print

<u>Tunnel #2</u>, 2003
Digital chromogenic print

Casebere studio with model,
New York City, 2005

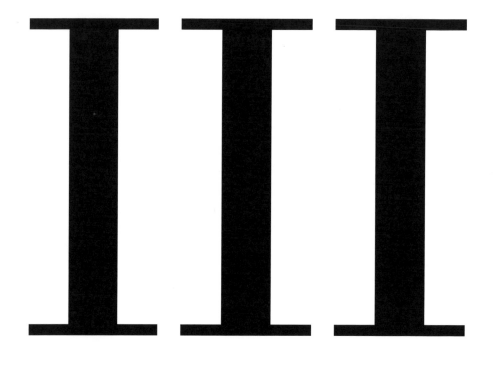

Practicing
After Taste

THE INTERIOR COMES HOME

Susan Yelavich

The desires and conceits entailed in the notion of "home" are becoming the lingua franca of the contemporary interior. Couches have migrated to bookstores, televisions populate doctors' offices, cushions double as library chairs, and offices are sprouting small cottages and huts. This elasticity in design typologies can be attributed to several recent developments, which I will elaborate on later in this essay. However, the public-private schism it heals (and sometimes conceals) was born in the larger history of modernism.

A succinct diagnosis of this split can be found in Mario Praz's *An Illustrated History of Interior Decoration: From Pompeii to Art Nouveau*—a valuable if often overlooked resource. Praz observed that:

> ...the ancients never lost sight of the proportions of the [room's] occupants, both people and the furniture...[but] the first modern Italian artists [having few extant pieces of furniture to emulate] had erroneously conceived everything according to a canon of magnificence, and for three centuries all of Europe...groaned slavishly under the weight of this error.[1]

The passage exposes the root of the divide between architecture and interior design—the historical circumstances that led to an artificial distinction between space and its physical membranes.

Mario Praz, who is better known as an Italian scholar of Romantic literature than he is for his contributions to the discussion of the interior, was specifically concerned with the deleterious impact of Renaissance scale on residential interiors. And while he never directly addresses the social structures that supported this "canon of magnificence," he does credit the reprise of the "domus" with the ascendancy of the bourgeoisie. Praz locates the recultivation of an atmosphere of *stimmung*, or intimacy, in seventeenth-century Dutch interiors. But he ultimately credits Robert Adam for advancing this ethos in the eighteenth century, arguing that his neoclassical ornament and furniture was most effective in modulating abstract space with the particularity of human scale.

I would like to suggest that we may be witnessing a similar phenomenon today as public interiors, traditionally aligned with the prestige of architectural space, are now taking their cues from residential interiors—spaces traditionally aligned with qualities considered secondary if not pejoratively feminine. Furthermore, the distinction between inside and outside, something Praz would have held firmly, has been weakening since the advent of the glass curtain wall, itself indebted to its interior-bound namesake.

Putting Praz's stylistic preferences and historic condition aside, his relevance to the conscientious designer lies in the premium he places on the personal interior, on qualities of proportion and intimacy that are not merely the sum of one's possessions. He sympathizes with the nineteenth-century aesthetician Walter Pater's observation that, "It might perhaps be that...things, as distinct from persons, such things as one had so abundantly around one, [had] come to be so much that the human being seemed suppressed and practically nowhere amid the objects he projected from himself."[2]

For Praz, this gluttony of possessions occludes the real potential of the interior, as a projection of the subject, or, in his view, the soul. And while it is unlikely that either Pater or Praz would be champions of the vernacular interiors that we see, for example, in Samuel Mockbee's houses in rural Alabama, to my mind both Pater and Praz offer an implicit endorsement of the subjective interior. Pater's use of the word "suppressed" specifically echoes my own response to interiors that are simply the sum of shopping lists without any self-confidence or, in fact, any awareness of the selves that might inhabit them.

A passage from Shirley Hazzard's novel, *The Transit of Venus*, illustrates what I mean. Here, Hazzard is describing how a callow young suitor reacts to the room he is received in by his future fiancée.

> The room itself appeared unawed by him—not from any disorder but from very naturalness. A room where there had been expectation would have conveyed the fact—by a tension of plumped cushions and placed magazines, a vacancy from unseemly objects bundled out of sight; by suspense slowly dwindling in the curtains. This room was without such anxiety. On its upholstery, the nap of the usual was undisturbed. No tribute of preparation had been paid him here, unless perhaps the flowers, which were fresh, and which he himself [would have brought] if he had only thought.[3]

The passage not only describes "the very naturalness" that so many interior designers say they want to achieve (and rarely do), it also offers a narrative of resistance to pressure from clients with preconceived agendas and also to preconceived protocols of design. It calls attention to the challenge and fragility of the everyday—something designers tend to freeze in the act of creating at the same time they are searching for tactics to rescue it (the illusive everyday) from the icebox of design strategy.

Chief among these tactics is the integration of memory and history with contemporary behaviors, technologies, and desires. And I see that integration occurring today through the reemergence of complexity, ornament, and craft to create iconoclastic interiors that reflect the personal and respond to the pleasures of the everyday. It is also apparent in the increasingly blurred lines between genders, something that the Dutch designer Petra Blaisse understands quite well. Blaisse is particularly deft at translating the memory and behavior of the curtain in contemporary spaces on a monumental scale. And she does it, not for reasons of nostalgia for grandiosity, but to create a counterpoint to the market mentality that drives so many of the spaces we occupy today. Her proscenium curtain for the Hackney Empire theater in London is a young girl's smocked dress writ large. **Fig. 1** Made of red velvet and gold rope, it respects the traditional theatrical convention demanded by the client and her own requirement— the intimation of human presence.

In another arena, health care, the British collective Muf Architecture/Art makes that presence felt quite literally. They screened the storefront window of the SureStart social agency in Surrey with aphorisms in Bengali script and English (Latinate) letters used in the languages of the people who avail themselves of the clinic's services. **Figs. 2, 3** The calligraphy becomes a lace curtain protecting the privacy of the clients while honoring them at the same time.

These two examples, however, are just one aspect of a Janus-faced proposition. On the bright side of this coin, we can see that the domestication of such environments provides more comfort, more reassurance, and more pleasure in domains once defined by prohibitions and exclusions. In fact, these kinds of changes are indebted to the social movements of the late 1960s and '70s that fought against barriers of race, class, gender, and physical ability and laid the groundwork for a larger climate of hospitality and accommodation.

Fig. 1
Proscenium curtain, Inside
Outside (Petra Blaisse),
Hackney Empire theater,
London, 2005
Courtesy of Inside Outside

But the dark side of the coin has everything to do with, well, coins—tender that is indifferent to place and identity, tender that makes personal transactions abstract. What does this have to do with interiors? I would argue that the erasure of boundaries between home and not-home is about persuading us to work longer, shop longer, and stay out longer and spend more. Add to the equation the recent millennial excess that reprised the home (in all its new incarnations from shop to office) as castle, replete with the psychic (and real) fortifications of the post-9/11 era. It seems the less time we spend at home the more we seek its comforts elsewhere. The signs of the domestic can equally be the signs of anxiety.

What about forces internal to design itself? Not coincidentally, at the same time that civil rights movements were opening closed doors (and spaces), the notion of history itself was being questioned by the critics of late modernism. The end of history, the end of utopias—so vaunted in the late-twentieth century—opened a Pandora's box of once forbidden forms. It was as if someone took a crowbar to the cast-iron floor of the Industrial Revolution and discovered the heart still beating in the corpus of the baroque and rococo. It is my argument that designers are increasingly drawn to torqued spaces and are less fearful of ornament because they resonate with the complicated nature of our own particular past-present. History is no longer understood as linear,

Figs. 2, 3
Storefront window, Muf
Architecture/Art, SureStart
social agency, Tower Hamlets
Health Authority Trust,
United Kingdom, 2000
Courtesy of Muf Architecture/Art
Photographs by Etienne Clement

but elliptical, like the spiral of DNA, with dominant and recessive genes that continually recombine. And where "the past" was off-limits, today all of history is available—including the history and legacy of modernism, which now is as much a part of our collective gene pool as the classicism on which it was based. In short, designers no longer have a script.

Compounding and complicating the situation even further are the inexorable tides of globalization and digital information. The *longue durée* has collapsed into a nanosecond and journeys that took months now are done with a click of a mouse. I cannot help but think that our latter-day gothic and profusion of arabesques may just have something to do with how often Arabic script appears on our news screens and the polyglot nature of our electronic urban lives. Moreover, these same qualities, once associated exclusively with the feminine and the "exotic" East, are a direct correlate of the algorithms that create our digital windows on the world. Of course, this raises the question of whether signs of the feminine, the decorative, and implicitly the "other" are being neutered or celebrated. I would argue that we are beginning to see the latter, since the attributes in question (e.g., perforations and folds) are still redolent with their primary sources (e.g., lace and drapery). To cite just two examples, the curved glass walls in OMA's Casa da Musica (2005) in Oporto, Portugal, are clearly frozen drapes; the walls and the furnishings of Marcel Wanders's Lute Suites hotel (2005) in Amsterdam are unabashedly lacy and floral even when they assume cartoon-like proportions. **Figs. 4, 5** We can also see serendipitous signs of this generation's "complexity and contradiction" in the cross-fertilization of interior typologies and the softening of their programs.[4] Today, health care facilities are increasingly adopting the language of spas and health clubs in their efforts to allay patients' fears and to be more responsive to their psychological needs. (For example, Buschow Henley Architects' Centre for Reproductive Medicine (2002) in London uses flowing white curtains and warm wood walls to alleviate the stress of fertility procedures.) At the same time, spas and health clubs are adopting the language of clinics to promote their services as essential to our physical and mental well-being. Civic spaces, from embassies to libraries to schools, are now designed to promote interaction and to mitigate their numbing bureaucracies. Offices are incorporating gyms and social spaces so workers can relax and recharge.

Fig. 4
OMA, Casa da Musica,
Oporto, Portugal, 2005
Courtesy of OMA
Photograph by Christian Richters

Fig. 5
Marcel Wanders Studio, Lute
Suites hotel, Amsterdam,
The Netherlands, 2005
Courtesy of Marcel Wanders
Studio
Photograph by Inga Powilleit

These elisions of public and private are certainly beneficial in their innate hospitality. To paraphrase the opening lines of Julieanna Preston's essay "Banter, Chit-chat and Sing-song," such border-crossing dialogues offer the opportunity to understand the lived environment as a spatial continuum.[5] Preston, of course, is dealing with the performative social nature of urban space and how it might inform the politics of control in the interior. Where she takes the macro view, I take the micro with a parallel concern that the benignity of "home" can also be used manipulatively.

Specifically, I am concerned about the dangers involved when the veneer of domesticity—the aura of *stimmung*, as Praz would say—is coopted to mask less positive agendas. In the office, this kind of design strategy is meant to soften the imposition of working longer hours; in the hospital, it runs the risk of infantilizing patients with empty signs of domesticity; and in spas and gyms, of suggesting that consumers really are patients, availing themselves of necessary treatments.

The problem of the domesticated interior may appear to be binary, but its interrogations can no longer be so, for design is a multivalent discipline. I remember a psychologist once carping that architects stole their theory from Lacanian psychology and French literary criticism, as if that were a problem. In fact, I think it would be strange not to use several sets of theoretical lenses to examine a realm that is by nature social, embracing manners, mores, behaviors, culture, gender, and race, not to mention the history of taste and aesthetics. Case in point, the art critic and curator Nicolas Bourriaud writes provocatively of a new aesthetic stance he calls "altermodernity." He describes it as "…a movement connected to the creolisation of cultures and the fight for autonomy, but also the possibility of producing singularities in a more and more standardized world."[6] I find his proposition enormously relevant to design. Programs such as that of the home and hospital may be creolized without devolving into arbitrary styling. Singularities that result from fully engaged conversations between client and designer are, in fact, possible. The Scottish Parliament building (2004) by EMBT Associates Architects is a superb example. Its concavities and convexities, supported by skewed timbers, produce a cogent asymmetry that aptly reflects the arguments at the heart of democratic governance. **Fig. 6**

But there is a discipline required of such ambition if it is not to devolve into heedless promiscuity. Extreme attentiveness is needed; not the fetishism of materials,

programs, or for that matter, of clients, who are at risk of being merely accommodated in late capitalist service industries like design. Attentiveness reveals opportunities for constructive particularity, not merely idiosyncrasy. Interiors that move beyond expectation and into material conversations—with time, with place, with people—accord a dignity to the rituals of the individuals and communities they serve.

But there is another dimension to attentiveness that has to do with the nature of practice itself. Interior designers tend to be orchestrators, not necessarily makers themselves. Nonetheless, the work of synthesis and coordination is also craft to be honed—a craft of responsivity to space and materials, to the designer's effects and the changes to preconceived plans made by the occupants of the space. In *The Craftsman*, sociologist Richard Sennett points out that in cognitive studies the ability to see thwarted expectations as opportunities for exploration is sometimes called "focal attention," an attention which in turn requires questioning, "physiologically dwelling in an incipient state [as] the pondering brain is considering its circuit options."[7] Sennett sees the third dimension of the craftsman—a figure that transcends gender and is concerned with working well—as the capacity to open up, "to draw unlike domains close to one another and to preserve tacit knowledge in the leap between them."[8] (For example, a wall woven with bands of coconut palm preserves the tacit knowledge of ancient reed-woven walls in a different material.[9])

Fig. 6
EMBT Associates Architects,
Scottish Parliament,
Edinburgh, Scotland, 2004
Photograph by Lewis Martin

The interior, with all its components from walls and floors to windows and furnishings—each with its own rich history, each with different associations to different people—presents designers with fulsome opportunities to attentively craft spaces for living that eschew the predictable for the personal. And if in the postmillennial moment, the personal became conflated with the domestic, with "home," might we now consider the excitement of leaving home as well as the comfort of staying at home? Both are intrinsic to our memories, both to living well in a cosmopolitan world—one that honors the self and honors others as well. An interior that materially hints at memories—and memories are always imperfect—recognizes its inhabitants and gives them something of themselves to recognize. Interiors that are crafted attentively engage the brain and the senses, making room for both to explore.

1 Mario Praz, *An Illustrated History of Interior Decoration: From Pompeii to Art Nouveau* (London: Thames & Hudson, 1987), 59–60.

2 Ibid., 65.

3 Shirley Hazzard, *The Transit of Venus* (New York: Penguin, 2000), 21.

4 The reference to "complexity and contradiction" is a nod to Robert Venturi and Denise Scott Brown's incorporation of the everyday urban landscape in their architecture, and to the title of Venturi's seminal book, *Complexity and Contradiction in Architecture*, first published by the Museum of Modern Art in New York in 1966.

5 Julieanna Preston, "Banter, Chit-chat and Sing-song: In-forming the Urban Concrete" in the *Proceedings of the 2006 ACSA West Regional Conference Surfacing Urbanisms*, Paulette Singley and Nick Roberts, convenors, Woodbury University, Pasadena, CA (2006), 201.

6 Nicolas Bourriaud, "Modern, Postmodern, Altermodern?" (keynote speech, Art Association of Australia & New Zealand Conference, University of Sydney, Australia, 2005. http://archive.artgallery.nsw.gov.au/aaanz05/abstracts/nicolas_bourriaud.

7 Richard Sennett, *The Craftsman* (New Haven, CT: Yale University Press, 2008), 278.

8 Ibid., 279.

9 "Palm Woven Paneling from Smith & Fong," *Architect's Newspaper*, November 14, 2007.

AN OLFACTORY RECONSTRUCTION OF PHILIP JOHNSON'S GLASS HOUSE INTERIOR

Jorge Otero-Pailos

Should the yellowish smoke stain that covers the ceiling of Philip Johnson's Glass House be cleaned, and the plaster made to look white again? Certainly for most people who (at least try to) keep their houses clean, it would seem desirable to steam clean it or simply paint over a ceiling if it is stained. But this is no ordinary house. It was built by a major American architect, and almost every detail in it has received the scrupulous attention of the best critics, historians, and students of architecture worldwide. I say almost because none of them paused to think about the staining of the ceiling, including Johnson it seems, for he didn't clean it once in the forty-seven years he lived there. Or perhaps none of them was prepared to think about that stain. To think about that stain as architecturally significant would necessarily lead us to ask whether knowledge of what caused it, an odoriferous combination of cigarette smoke and poor ventilation, is essential to our understanding of the building and its interior, and of what makes it important. As I would like to argue, to consider historic smells in the equation of architectural significance involves calling into question a series of fundamental assumptions about how we define, interpret, and understand the authenticity of architectural interiors, and to include the kinds of evidence, such as stains, that our best minds tend to edit out for no other reason, perhaps, than we lack a coherent analytical framework within which to put it.

To be sure, this is not the kind of glorious natural stain that architects like to romanticize about as "weathering." This is a mean cigarette smoke stain that in our smoke-free-interiors world evokes all sorts of negative connotations, from tar and foul odor, to pollution and cancer. Why should anyone like to preserve it? One possible argument is that it constitutes undeniable evidence not only of the changing lifestyles of American society, and of what was considered socially acceptable, but also, and more importantly for the purposes of architectural history and preservation, of our changing architectural aesthetics of olfaction. Granted the stain itself does not smell. It is a deposit of the smelly airborne particulates that once filled the house. Today it is only a visual trace, but it is a valuable permanent clue to understanding the more ephemeral aesthetics of olfaction, and without it, expanding the interpretation of the interior to include a discussion of olfaction would seem arbitrary. Our knowledge of Johnson's aesthetics of olfaction is inversely proportional to what has been written about his visual aesthetics, a fact that reflects the state of these two fields more

Interior, living area, Philip
Johnson, Glass House, 1949
The Carnegie Arts of the United
States collection, ARTstor

generally. Indeed, to focus on olfaction is to call for a revision of the methods and ambitions of both architectural history and preservation, such as the emphasis both place on the original architect's visual intentions as the gold standard for evaluating the importance of buildings.

The answer to whether to clean the stain does not, or should not, hinge entirely on our knowledge of Johnson's olfactory intentions. After many years of withstanding heavy criticisms from poststructuralists, preservation seems ready to move beyond the narrow directive that only those things that reflect the (ever elusive) intentions of the architect should be preserved in a building. Yet moving preservation toward the opposite extreme of keeping everything that ever happened to a building would render it aesthetically meaningless. The debate about whether to clean the Glass House ceiling suggests a new problem and therefore a new direction: making the decision to preserve requires that we expand how we deem things architecturally significant, from focusing on the original stated visual aesthetic intentions to including unintentional aesthetics, which in this case involve primarily questions of olfaction.

The architectural significance of the smoke stain rests on the ability to present it as a key piece of evidence in the story of the building's intentional *and* unintentional aesthetics. By unintentional aesthetics I do not mean Johnson's design mistakes or some spurious notion of reading his unconscious pathologies. Rather, very simply, the term refers to those aesthetic dimensions of the interior that were not explicitly designed by Johnson, but that were nonetheless set into motion by his design, and developed over time through the action of other creative agents (meaning people and nonhuman agents too). Whereas intentional aesthetics can be bracketed to a discrete moment of creation, unintentional aesthetics unfold in a more dilated and not necessarily sequential temporality, best described as counterfactual, in the sense that it is irreducible to any one moment in time. In order to apprehend the unintentional aesthetics of a building, we must situate ourselves vis-à-vis these multiple temporalities simultaneously, and consider them in relation to one another, without giving one primacy over the other. This is counterfactual from the point of view of bodily experience, which naturally tends to give more weight to the lived present, and requires a supplementary mental act of projection. In practice, in order to grasp the unintentional aesthetics of an interior, visitors need cues that invite them to do the necessary mental work of looking upon their material environment, not simply as the representation of any one particular moment, present or past, but rather as a register of many overlapping, coexisting, and sometimes also contradictory temporal processes. This is something that is very hard to do through architectural history, because writing is experienced linearly, and because it is by definition a selective representation of the building. Perhaps Walter Benjamin came the closest to successfully using the written word to depict unintentional architectural aesthetics in his famously unfinished Arcades Project, with its exploration of montage and collage as historiographical methods. By contrast to architectural history, preservation benefits from the fact that it is a direct physical intervention on the very material substrate of both intentional and unintentional aesthetics. The tendency up to the present has been to intervene in architectural works in such a way as to enhance, for lack of a better word, the original visual intentional aesthetics precisely by erasing, or downplaying, the unintentional aesthetics of the building.

In 2008, after a series of discussions with the curators and staff of the Glass House about how the ongoing conservation work would impact future interpretations, I proposed to the National Trust for Historic Preservation an olfactory reconstruction of three moments in the Glass House, 1949, 1959, and 1969. My proposal was an experimental solution to the problems that overemphasis on visual intentional aesthetics create for interpretation: we produced olfactory cues, smell reconstructions of the house at various points in time, that oriented the visitor toward the unintentional aesthetics of the interior (e.g., the stained ceiling, the crackling wood varnishes, the damaged leather) and provided them with the necessary experiential context to grasp them as a meaningful part of a broader aesthetic program that was more architecturally significant for being both intentional and unintentional. The project also explored the thesis that any act of preservation is precisely the ability to relate intentional and unintentional aesthetics in a meaningful way, thus freeing preservation design from the tired self-effacing search for an authenticity based on architectural originality, while simultaneously cultivating an alternative mode of creativity, which unlike new construction was not beholden to the fetishism of perpetual stylistic newness.

The smells were to be delivered by a series of six square floor odor diffusers that were to sit next to and visually match the cylindrical can lights on the floor of the Glass House. To create this work I was fortunate to work with Rosendo Mateu, perfumer and

Interior, living area, Philip
Johnson, Glass House, 1949
Ezra Stoller Archive, ARTstor

head of Puig Perfumery Center, and to learn from the great knowledge of the Carolina Herrera fragrances team. Mateu was trained as a chemist and forged his career in the laboratories of Antonio Puig in Barcelona, later apprenticing with master noses such as Marcel Carles and Arturo Jordi Pey of Firmenich. The project benefited from the Puig archive of smells, one of the most important in the world, which stores over twenty thousand elements of smell—almost the entirety of scents manufactured in the twentieth century. Each archived smell is associated with a textual description of its olfactive notes, indexed by seven descriptors and registered in a digital database. There are about one thousand descriptors ranging from the narrow to the open-ended, such as food, environmental smells, sensations, and other olfactory analogies, as well as chemical products. Typical descriptors include words like humidity, sea, pastry, recently baked bread, chocolate, hospital, tar, barber shop, rubber, electrical smells, school, various flowers, woods, resins, spices, milk, wine, pencil, lipstick, metallic, mineral, ozone, burnt, sweat, and oxygen. These descriptors were the first step in the research required to locate particular concentrates, which eventually formed the olfactory profile of our reconstruction.

The reconstruction itself is composed of three distinct aromas layered onto one another that are meant to be smelled in sequence, providing a compressed experience of the first two decades of the Glass House. The first recreates the smell of the new house when it was built in 1949. It is a blend of newly lacquered wood closets, newly painted steel, fresh plaster from the ceiling, cement mortar from the floor, and a hint of leather from the new Barcelona chairs and the bathroom ceiling. It is composed of terpinolene, beta-pinene, and trementine combined with oleates and also conveys a sensation of humidity, notes of mold, and wet earth.

The second aroma reconstructs the aesthetic of olfaction preferred by sophisticated American men of the mid to late 1950s. It is a blend of the most popular eaux de cologne of the time, including Old Spice, Canoe, English Lavender, and Acqua Velva. It is composed of lavender, bergamot, rosewood, lemon, geranium, clove, amber, and tobacco. This scent introduces the human element into the reconstruction, which was central to the experience of the house. Johnson regularly hosted New York's male architectural elite at the Glass House for private conversations.

The third aroma recreates the smell of the house in the late 1960s, by which point its porous surfaces had become impregnated with the smoke of thousands of

Philip Johnson and Andy
Warhol inside the Glass
House, ca. 1960s
Courtesy of David McCabe

cigarettes and cigars, especially the plaster ceiling. It is composed of a mix of absolutes of dry leaves of tobacco with pure cigar effect, black tobacco and tobacco from Bulgaria, scents of smoke and incense, burnt logs, aged leather, and wood.

Taken together, these three aromatic layers represent our first experimental steps toward a preservation science of olfactory reconstruction. To those familiar with the existing scholarship on the Glass House and with traditional preservation practices, this experimental project might seem out of place, or at least counterintuitive. Although the Glass House has not ceased to be in the public eye since it was built in 1949, there are no public accounts of its smell. The first publication on the Glass House appeared in September 1949 in *Life* magazine. The article focused on the layout of the house, pointing out that it was one large room without interior partitions.[1] Two months later, it was published in *Architectural Forum* with a special emphasis on its choice of materials.[2] In 1950, Johnson offered his account of the formal precedents of the design in "House at New Canaan, Connecticut," which appeared in *Architectural Review* and was received as somewhat of a provocation to modernist architects who tended to be less open about their debts to history.[3] A steady stream of articles followed during the next quarter of a century mostly debating Johnson's own analysis of the house's visual composition. By 1975, the American Institute of Architects awarded the building its prestigious twenty-five-year award.[4] In 1979, the Johnson House entered the canon of American architectural history as the Glass House, appearing in textbooks such as Leland Roth's *A Concise History of American Architecture*. Students who had never set foot in the building nevertheless came to know its appearance inside out: the fifty-six-by-thirty-two-foot floor plan, the eight perimeter black steel columns, the famous corner detail of the eight-inch I-section column, the six-foot wood closets dividing the space, the herringbone brick floor, the cylindrical bathroom-cum-fireplace, the elevations with central doors and eighteen-foot-wide inoperable single-pane plate glass windows, which Johnson ordered especially without a manufacturer's logo. From the 1970s to the '90s, the discipline's brightest minds interpreted the building, slowly interlacing their analyses of the house's formal precedents with the political history and uses of those precedents. Worthy of note are the studies by Kenneth Frampton, Peter Eisenman, Vincent Scully, Robert A. M. Stern, Jeffrey Kipnis, and Kazys Varnelis, who was the most daring in raising questions about Johnson's own politics and his infamous prewar sympathy for Nazi ideology.[5] More recently, scholars have focused on the debts owed by Johnson to various collaborators who had helped design the appearance of house, such as lighting designer Richard Kelly.[6] In sum, during the last sixty years a corpus of scholarship has grown around the visual dimensions of the Glass House and its role in the social politics of architecture. But we lack documentation about the house's odors, or how they were managed, ventilated, and perfumed. Through the filter of available scholarship, as with most architectural records, the Glass House appears distorted into an odorless image of a glass house.

Preservation operations often have the unfortunate tendency of slowly transforming buildings into the documents that describe them. The image of the Glass House depicted in its scholarship is therefore critical, and especially now, as it is currently undergoing its most important transformation since it was built, from a private house into a public museum. Johnson himself initiated this transformation in 1986, when he donated the house and the necessary funds to maintain it to the National Trust for Historic Preservation. A resident curator moved to the property at that time, although Johnson and his partner David Whitney continued to live in the house until their deaths in 2005. Two years later, the estate, which comprises the Glass House, eight other buildings, a designed landscape, and a sizable art collection, opened for the first time to the public. Visually, it reveals itself today essentially as Johnson and Whitney left it. But the house's smell has already changed dramatically. The absence of a written olfactory record means that little attention will be devoted to the preservation of the olfactory aesthetics in vogue during the house's period of significance.

Despite the lacuna of written documents about the house's smell, the house itself bears physical marks of its olfactory aesthetics, especially on the surfaces that were difficult to clean and maintain. The plaster ceiling is one of those key pieces of evidence. Once pure white, it is now yellowed by thousands of cigarettes smoked below it. We therefore know that the air in the Glass House was regularly vitiated with airborne particles of tar—the house is notoriously cumbersome to ventilate, as there are no operable windows and one must open the door to allow air to circulate. Another example is the leather ceiling tiles in the bathroom that have partially peeled off, indicating a combination of humidity and lack of ventilation, both determinant factors in olfaction. In addition to these physical records, we know that construction materials

(overleaf)
Philip Johnson, Glass House,
1949
The Carnegie Arts of the United
States collection, ARTstor

release particular smell signatures—paints, lacquers, and varnishes, as well as the woods, leathers, and textiles used throughout the house and blended together into a unique mixture that was constantly changing depending on the surface area of each material and environmental factors such as temperature, humidity, ventilation, and solar radiation. These physical traces, environmental conditions, and material properties provided the basis for our reconstruction.

Significantly, glass is odorless. One of the questions raised by this reconstruction of the house's historical smells is whether Johnson's naming of the building embodied both his visual *and* olfactory aesthetic ambitions. His frustration with the mirroring effects of glass, especially at night, have been amply documented as signs of failure.[7] More research is required to understand whether he intended his Glass House to be an entirely unscented environment and whether he also considered its odors a failure. Johnson's personal correspondence is slowly becoming accessible to scholars and we can expect some advances to be made on this front. Also, the oral history project currently being undertaken by the National Trust for Historic Preservation can reveal important facts—keeping in mind that what an interviewee attends to during an interview has a great deal to do with the questions asked.

Whether or not Johnson was intentionally considering olfactory aesthetics, his design was influenced by architects, such as Ledoux, whose fame came partly from the fact that he was a pioneer in a new aesthetics of olfaction, although twentieth-century architectural historians mostly obviated this fact, focusing instead on his visual forms. In his famous 1950 essay citing the precedents for the house, Johnson stated that "The cubic, 'absolute' form of my glass house and the separation of functional units into two absolute shapes rather than a major and minor massing of parts comes directly from Ledoux, the eighteenth-century father of modern architecture."[8] Based on functional considerations, Johnson divided the house into two "absolute shapes," indeed two pavilions, one with a glass envelope, the other with a brick enclosure, facing each other and slightly offset. But what functional considerations was Johnson really concerned with? Both buildings have bedrooms, bathrooms, closets, and writing desks. The functional separation had more to do with distinguishing between users than uses. The glass house was Johnson's space and the brick house the space of visitors. Guests, their smells and their noises, were segregated and contained in a separate building.

Johnson's invocation of Ledoux may offer an important clue regarding the house's unintentional olfactory aesthetics. For Ledoux, the ability of individuals to be housed in separate well-ventilated rooms was both a physical and moral therapeutic imperative. Ledoux was obsessed with the purity of air in buildings and their autonomy was dictated, in part, by ventilation needs. In his ideal town at Chaux, he separated houses and public buildings into pavilions that could be individually aired. Historian Alain Corbin has shown how Ledoux's development of the pavilion form was part of a larger European cultural moment in which specialists in every field fought foul smells in order to stem the spread of disease.[9] In the eighteenth century and much of the nineteenth century, before Pasteur's proof that disease was not transmitted by foul air but by odorless microorganisms, social reformers identified bad smells as signs and bearers of morbidity. In the late eighteenth century, scientists like Jean-Godefroy Léonhardy, Antoine Lavoisier, Joseph Priestley, and Karl Wilhelm Scheele "passionately collected, decanted, confined and preserved 'airs'—also called gases—and located the effects of each on the animal organism."[10] They established taxonomies of "respirable airs" and stinking emanations, eventually leading to the discovery that air was not an element but a mixture of gases—these collections of "airs" were the precursors of today's smell archives and important sources in the evolution of contemporary perfumery. Other people's sweat and exhalations were thought to be a potential source of contagion.

The notion of atmospheric isolation first found architectural expression in military barracks and new hospital designs such as those of Julien-David Le Roy, who proposed an individual outlet at the head of each bed, protecting patients from the smell (i.e., the diseases) of others.[11] Harkening back to this late-eighteenth-century architectural moment, Johnson described the plan of his brick pavilion as baroque (and Miesian at the same time), calling attention to the shape and location of the individual windows: they are located at the head of each guest bed.

By the hygienic standards of the 1940s, Johnson's twin pavilion scheme for his house had significant benefits. It is worth recalling that at that time most Americans still feared each other's exhalations, since they were identified as vehicles for the transmission of tuberculosis. Part of the popular interest in international style modernism came from the advances of modern architects in well-ventilated sanatoria. American architects studied precedents and advances in the design of tuberculosis sanatoria from around the world. Alvar Aalto's Paimio Sanatorium (1929–33) in Finland became particularly famous, but also significant was that of José Villagran Garcia (1936) in Huipulco, Mexico, and the Zonnestraal Sanatorium by Johannes Duiker and Bernard Bijvoet (1928–30) in Hilversum, The Netherlands.

Clearly, Johnson's interest in individual isolation also had a narcissistic dimension. He did, after all, choose to seclude himself, alone in his pavilion, yet to publicly display himself (yes, his neighbors complained) behind a glass enclosure more typical of commercial storefronts. Whereas Johnson presented his image publicly (hiding his guests away behind brick), he carefully confined breathable air and personal emanations into the private realm. According to historian Paul Metzner, the deliberate construction of the self as the simultaneous coincidence of and separation between public and private life also has its origins in the late eighteenth century. During the time of Ledoux, the life of common citizens started to become divided into two distinct spheres, private and public. What held these two spheres together was a romantic notion of self-centeredness, perfected by figures like Rousseau, who was known for being simultaneously reclusive and ambitious. According to Metzner, "Self-love manifested itself in the private sphere as a drive for the exclusion of others and in the public sphere as a drive for recognition by others."[12] This ideal of self-centeredness became the identifying psychological trait on which the emerging nineteenth-century bourgeoisie built its ideal of the autonomous individual. Viewed from the outside, the glass pavilion was all about Johnson's public figure. From the inside, the wraparound glass afforded the privilege of private 360-degree views into the landscape, which Johnson famously referred to with the sobriquet "expensive wallpaper."

By focusing on the precedents of Johnson's unintentional aesthetics of olfaction we arrive at an analysis of the Glass House that enriches previous visual analyses. We can appreciate more clearly the relationship between the choice of dividing the house into two pavilions and Johnson's taste for bourgeois self-fashioning, without falling into the trap of identifying the architectural type of the pavilion with the social type of the bourgeois. After all, the pavilion type itself is not what reflects a bourgeois sensitivity. Rather, it is the way the two pavilions were used to separate users and the narcissistic-voyeuristic employment of glass.

The larger issue to consider here is what we know about Johnson's life and aesthetic intentions can help us understand his house better, but it can also lead our interpretations astray. This is true with any architect, but especially with Johnson, who was an infamous manipulator of his own history and thought nothing of deauthorizing the documents of his own past.[13] Buildings are both much more and far less than what their original architects intended. They have a life that the first architects cannot control. If they stand for more than a few decades they will invariably be maintained, completed, improved, or mangled by subsequent generations of users, builders, and architects, whose creative work is often disregarded by historians that choose to reduce the life of architecture to the moment when the first architect was involved. Returning to the previous discussion, the historiographical bias of original intentionality is linked to the partiality of many architectural historians toward the visual. The pragmatic reality is that scholars base their work on the documents that are available about buildings and those are mostly visual. But that does not mean that architects were not concerned with the other senses, it was simply a function of the technological limitations of media. During the first twenty years of the Glass House's existence, media technology changed dramatically. In 1949 Richard Neutra still had to translate his interest in the sound and smell of architecture into words.[14] But by the late 1960s, advances in micro-encapsulation made it possible for architects like Doug Michels, Chip Lord, and other members of the Ant Farm collective to communicate their design ambitions with "scratch and sniff" stickers.[15] The exhibition *Sugerencias Olfativas* held at the Fundació Joan Miró in 1978 showcased the work of Rosendo Mateu as part of a larger exploration of new advances in the artistry and technology of smell. As a result of that exhibition a larger set of architects became aware of the possibilities for designing the olfactory aesthetics of environments and communicating their work through scented books. The olfactory reconstruction presented here follows in that tradition, extending it to the discipline of preservation.

Preservation creativity is never *ex nihilo*. It is always a response to a human product that precedes it and to the history of interpretations of that product. The preservation of the Glass House must respond to the particular material conditions of that building and confront the various biases of previous interpretations, such as the emphasis on the visual to the exclusion of all the other senses and of the primacy of place given to Johnson's intentions. As Manfredo Tafuri noted, preservation work can put scholarship in crisis, by confronting it with the reality of the building itself and presenting it with new material evidence that may challenge previous assumptions.[16]

This particular work of olfactory preservation also confronts preservation scholarship itself, which is mute on the subject of smell. Despite the technical sophistication of the perfume industry, there is a dearth of serious attempts at historical reconstructions of smells. Rather, like architectural historians, preservationists have tended to approach the subject of historical reconstructions primarily as a visual problem. The degree of a reconstruction's integrity, for instance, is commonly evaluated visually on the basis of stylistic accuracy (especially in the case of works of high architecture), or fidelity to the extant evidence of drawings and photographs. Rather than to posit a rare form of professionally induced anosmia to explain the double exclusion of smell from historical analyses of the Glass House and from the discourse on reconstruction, I would suggest that the key to comprehending the moment that discourse has fallen silent is to be found in our contemporary aesthetics of olfaction.

Although the subject of old house smells rarely comes up in professional architectural or preservation journals, the popular press is obsessed with it. Judging by real estate literature, when Americans purchase homes they are driven as much by olfaction as by the looks of a place. Realtors warn sellers to "clean and air out any musty smelling areas. Odors are a no-no."[17] More bluntly, they set out rules such as "play down the scent" and "play up the visual."[18] Americans, it seems, value odorless homes. More importantly for our purposes, they negatively associate old buildings with a foul stench. The smell of old cigarette smoke is thought to be particularly noxious. "A friend of mine just bought a lovely 1920s house," wrote a concerned journalist in a recent issue of *House Beautiful*, "but it has layers of old smells, especially from fireplaces and tobacco. How can she get rid of them?"[19] The notion of "old smells" is marked negatively as something dead. The stale stench of smoke is relegated to the past and deemed something to be expunged in order to restore the house to its "lovely" 1920s state.

Should the Glass House be restored to its "lovely" 1949 state? To do so would require cleaning the yellow stains on the plaster ceiling. The theory that restoration should be a cleaning operation has evolved out of a series of instrumental misreadings of Viollet-le-Duc, who thought of restoration as a profoundly modern operation. In 1843 he wrote that "To restore a building, is not to preserve it, to repair, or rebuild it; it is to reinstate it in a condition of completeness that could never have existed at any given time."[20] This sentence, quoted so often in isolation, has led commentators to boil down Viollet-le-Duc's theory to the idea that restoration is the operation of removing later accretions and adding missing parts to achieve historic buildings with stylistic integrity. In truth however, Viollet-le-Duc not only tolerated later accretions but vehemently defended their retention, so long as they were innovations in building technology that improved the building's performance and were unavailable in previous periods. For instance, he was in favor of maintaining a thirteenth-century cornice gutter on a twelfth-century building, because the cornice gutter was a technological innovation of the thirteenth century without which the roof of an old building would have collapsed. Viollet-le-Duc employed an admittedly structuralist/rationalist analytical framework for determining whether accretions should be kept or removed. The point is that his restorations did not aim exclusively at achieving stylistic unity. They endeavored instead to faithfully capture buildings as continuous sites of innovation, restricted by their given material conditions but open-ended as far as time. The fact that Viollet-le-Duc did not identify a building's state of completeness with a particular moment in time has led architectural historian Aron Vinegar to interpret his theory of restoration as a precursor of the contemporary theory that preservation is as much a material as a temporal practice, best described in the tense of the future anterior.[21] In sum, restoration does not necessarily require the removal of material accretions in favor of visual or stylistic integrity. It does mean, however, that the basis for removing or retaining elements, even the soot on the ceiling, must be explicitly articulated and theorized.

To be explicit, then, removing the material traces of the smells that permeated Johnson's Glass House, such as the yellow tint of the plaster ceiling, would be to restore the house according to the olfactory bias of contemporary society. In the 1950s, the stale smell of cigarette smoke was a socially acceptable aesthetic in elite environments. Today, it is associated with lower-class environments. To restore the Glass House as a deodorized pavilion would certainly make it easier for contemporary visitors to grasp its elite nature. Preservation is often rightly accused of distorting historical evidence in order to advance myth and folkloric tales—of the very sort that Johnson liked to spin about himself.[22] Preservation can also be a critical practice that questions its own modus operandi and nudges other disciplines to rethink their assumptions about it. Our experimental reconstruction of the smells of the Glass House was designed not as an attempt to return to a more authentic, undistorted past, but as the introduction of a necessary contemporary artificiality that would cue visitors to grasp the interior as both a work of intentional and unintentional aesthetics, making the building a much richer and significant work of architecture precisely because it is irreducible to the figure of Johnson. We did not obtain approval from the National Trust to install it. There is no question that the smells might be offensive to contemporary visitors. Yet it is this difference between our aesthetic sensibilities and those impregnated in the Glass House that make it a perfect place to reopen the question of the sociology of smell, unintentional aesthetics and their lasting if unrecognized influence on our understanding of interior.

A version of this article was previously published as "An Olfactory Reconstruction of Philip Johnson's Glass House," in *AAFiles*, no. 57 (2008): 40–45. I would like to thank the editor Tom Weaver for his permission to republish it. I would also like to thank Kent Kleinman and Joanna Merwood-Salisbury for their insightful comments and suggestions.

1   "Glass House," *Life* (September 1949): 94–96.

2   "Glass House," *Architectural Forum* (November 1949): 74–79.

3   Philip Johnson, "House at New Canaan, Connecticut," *Architectural Review* (September 1950): 152–59.

4   "Honor Awards go to Nine Buildings, the 25-year Award to a Glass House," *American Institute of Architects Journal*, no. 5 (May 1975): 26–43.

5   Kenneth Frampton, "The Glass House Revisited," *Institute for Architecture and Urban Studies Catalogue*, no. 9 (1978): 38–59; Peter Eisenman and Philip Johnson, "Peter Eisenman's Interview with Philip Johnson [and] Oriental Pavilion, New Canaan, Connecticut, 1991–1993," *Zodiac*, no. 9 (March–August 1993): 134–49; Vincent Scully, "Architecture: Philip Johnson: The Glass House Revisited," *Architectural Digest* (November 1986): 116–25, 220; Robert A. M. Stern, "The Evolution of Philip Johnson's Glass House, 1947–48," *Oppositions*, no. 10 (Fall 1977): 56–67; Jeffrey Kipnis, "Philip Johnson," *A + U: Architecture and Urbanism* (April 1992): 6–39; Kazys Varnelis, *The Spectacle of the Innocent Eye: Vision, Cynical Reason and the Discipline of Architecture in Postwar America* (Ph.D. Dissertation, Cornell University, 1994).

6   Margaret Maile Petty, "Illuminating the Glass Box: The Lighting Designs of Richard Kelly," *Journal of the Society of Architectural Historians* 66, no. 2 (2007): 194–219.

7   Ibid.

8   Johnson, "House at New Canaan, Connecticut," 154.

9   Alain Corbin, *The Foul and the Fragrant: Odor and the French Social Imagination* (Cambridge, MA: Harvard University Press, 1986).

10 Ibid., 15.

11 Richard Etlin, "L'air dans l'urbanisme des lumières," in *Dix-Huitième Siècle Paris*, no. 9 (1977): 123–34. These early experiments later influenced the design of prison cells in the nineteenth century, thoroughly analyzed by Michel Foucault in *Discipline and Punish: The Birth of the Prison*, trans. Alan Sheridan (New York: Vintage Books, 1977).

12 Paul Metzner, *Crescendo of the Virtuoso: Spectacle, Skill and Self-Promotion in Paris during the Age of Revolution* (Berkeley, CA: University of California Press, 1998).

13 Leslie Klein, "History, Autobiography and Interpretation: The Challenge of Philip Johnson's Glass House," *Future Anterior* 1, no. 2 (2004): 59–66.

14 Richard J. Neutra, "The Sound and Smell of Architecture," *Progressive Architecture* (November 1949): 65–66.

15 Felicity D. Scott, *Living Archive 7: Ant Farm* (Barcelona: Actar, 2008).

16 Manfredo Tafuri, Bruno Pedretti, and Chiara Baglione, "Storia, Conservazione, Restauro," *Casabella* 55, no. 580 (1991): 23–26, 60–61. See also Andrew Leach, "Libido Operandi or Conflict: Tafuri on Historic Preservation and Historiography," *Future Anterior* 3, no. 2 (Winter 2006): 1–9.

17 Elizabeth Weintraub, "How to Prepare your House for Sale," About.com website, accessed September 1, 2008, http://homebuying.about.com/od/sellingahouse/ht/homeprep.htm.

18 Elizabeth Weintraub, "Top 10 Home Showing Tips," About.com website, accessed September 1, 2008, http://homebuying.about.com/od/sellingahouse/qt/ShowingHome.htm.

19 Eve M. Kahn, "Maintenance and Odor Removal Q&A," *House Beautiful* (June 2008): 64.

20 M. F. Hearn, ed., *The Architectural Theory of Viollet-le-Duc: Readings and Commentary* (Cambridge, MA: MIT Press, 1990), 269.

21 Aron Vinegar, "Viollet-le-Duc and Restoration in the Future Anterior," *Future Anterior* 3, no. 2 (2006): 55–65. Vinegar maintains that Viollet-le-Duc conceived of buildings as entities with paradoxically "untimely" temporalities. He argues that Viollet-le-Duc's conception of time was "implicated": "a time that is not over there in 'segments'—a set of discrete temporal units following each other as successive moments in a line or sequence organized in relationship to a distant and stable 'present'—but rather a time that we are part of, involved in, caught up in the midst of, but which we never quite master and are thus also apart from."

22 David Lowenthal, "Fabricating Heritage," *History & Memory* 10, no. 1 (1998), http://www.iupjournals.org/history/ham10-1.html.

Interview with Constance Adams: We Are in This Thing Together

Constance Adams is a specialist in high-performance architecture and design innovation, particularly in the area of architecture for human spaceflight. Her work as a consultant to the National Aeronautics and Space Administration (NASA) and commercial space ventures has sensitized her to issues of human-machine interface, sustainable systems, the importance of biomimetic design, and the issue of risk in the design and building professions. Adams's work at NASA consists of a unique portfolio of designs for the human spaceflight program, such as two surface habitats for lunar/Mars exploration and a long-duration crew transit spacecraft, as well as operations planning and integration for space missions including the International Space Station (ISS). She spoke with Kent Kleinman in Houston in July 2009.

Kent Kleinman: You were trained as an architect, worked for one of the finest postwar architects, Kenzo Tange, and honed your craft in two extraordinarily refined building cultures, Germany and Japan. How did you come to choose NASA and Houston as your professional context?

Constance Adams: I was visiting my father and stepmother in Dallas in the mid-1990s, and I figured that while I was in Texas I might as well go down to the Johnson Space Center (JSC). I took a little trolley through and it went past all of these nondescript buildings. At the time, the Smithsonian hadn't yet restored the Saturn V, so it was just this garden tchotchke lying out there in the grass! What was, and still is, breathtaking to me about the facilities that we work in at JSC is how basic they are, yet the absolute edge of the envelope is represented by this place. And I thought that the one thing more incredible than participating in the reconstruction of Berlin would be designing a human settlement for another planet. So I wrote a note to a friend of a friend who worked at NASA saying that it would be incredible to work for you and a year later, I got an email asking if I wanted the job. They interviewed me to design the BIO-Plex, to do the interior outfitting.

KK: BIO-Plex? Please describe it because most people won't know what it is.

> **CA:** It stands for BIOlogical-regenerative-life-support-systems-test-comPLEX. It was to be a complex of ISS modules, fourteen-foot diameter cylinders in a horizontal configuration. Outside of the habitat chamber was a module where wheat would be planted for food, and another where bacteria would be grown that were able to cleanse the water. There was a precursor, a much more rudimentary facility, doing preliminary testing when I arrived in mid-1997. A crew of four people spent ninety days in this chamber to test integrated biological systems. For the test sponsors, who were life support engineers, the crew members were just metabolic loads. But I was able to squeeze a sociological study in there: we taped a continuous loop observing what spaces the crew used inside this volume and how much time they spent socializing as opposed to being alone. For the first time, I became a scientist. I started constructing designs for BIO-Plex and other analog habitats, that would allow me to test different questions. We did all these studies about how one could make the best use of a horizontal cylinder in any kind of gravity environment. Of course, using a horizontal cylinder is incredibly wasteful in terms of your usable floor area if you're in a gravity environment. But when you're in a space station, you're not in gravity.

KK: Clearly parameters that are taken for granted for terrestrial designers are variables in your context. Let's define the role of gravity in your world of design.

> **CA:** Moon is one-sixth g. Mars is half the size of Earth, and has a third of the gravity. We call these conditions variable gravity, or planetary gravity, or surface gravity environments. Basically the only three surface environments that we can really imagine designing for

at this point are one-sixth g, one-third g, and one g: the moon, Mars, and Earth.

KK: When I read the word "microgravity" we're talking about the gravitational condition of orbiting vessels?

> **CA:** What people call zero-g, we call microgravity because every-thing with mass has at least a little gravity. Also, there are other forces acting on us all the time that can quasi simulate gravity. We're designing experiments to be conducted inside an orbiting vehicle and if it requires complete zero-g and somebody flushes a toilet or gets on the treadmill, you may have just screwed up an experiment!

Astronaut Gerald P. Carr, commander of the Skylab 4 mission, demonstrates weight training in zero-gravity by balancing Astronaut William R. Pogue on his finger.

You need to make a note that a force has been exerted that might be mistaken for a gravitational vector. But humans require a gravity vector to function properly—whether that means in terms of perception or in terms of metabolism. The secret structural component of our bodies is the gravity vector.

KK: So there is a physiological dimension to gravity. Our perception of the world and our organizational systems are synchronized with gravity.

CA: Yes, with gravity and with time. What plays a role is not only the size of the planet that you're on, but also the amount of time required to get there. It's three days to the moon. The moon is one-sixth g. We're Superman on the moon. We're *too* Superman. We're falling over on our faces because we're much too strong. But it is six months from here to Mars, and our bodies will deteriorate during the zero-g phase of the flight, no matter how much exercise we're getting during the trip. We're probably not Superman on Mars. We're probably just about okay. The body is a variable. We know that the body deteriorates very quickly. We don't know how quickly it catches back up again. Metabolism plays an important role. The fact is that the body's exchange of internal energies actually causes it to metabolize the musculoskeletal system over time without gravity.

KK: This raises a question about proprioception, especially in a state of suspension.

CA: It makes me laugh a great deal in yoga class when they say "just imagine that you are floating." The truth is: when you are floating you don't feel that you are floating. You don't feel anything. You cannot imagine it. We imagine floating like flying, like skydiving or bungee jumping. But this is inaccurate because you have a force acting on you. The most important thing is the *feelinglessness*. The body without the gravity vector doesn't have inherent feeling. In the crew quarters they were sleeping vertically pinned to the wall, but they didn't sleep very well if they weren't strapped down because it is really nice to have a blanket stay on top of you when you sleep. Relaxation involves the relationship of the body to some other surface. You're stretching out on that surface. It involves the gravity vector.

KK: The role of the horizon in shaping our built environment and ordering the natural world is fundamental, both physiologically and culturally. The Cartesian gridding of space is intimately related to the presence of gravity, and the trope of the horizontal versus the vertical is a cultural construct of enormous range and power. The very notion of a plan, and the making of plans, is related to the conception of a principal plane of action. Without a horizon we could not organize perspectival space. And the cultural association of verticality with power and vitality and the supine with submission and death is pervasive and basic to so much cultural activity. In the gravity-bound world, the diagonal is a liminal state, a transitory condition.

Astronaut Mike Fossum
sleeps in his sleeping bag,
attached to the middeck
lockers of the space shuttle
Discovery.

In space, however, the suspended body—the non-orthogonal as a natural and ordinary state—seems to upend all this cultural baggage and all this gravity-bound geometry. How does this extraordinary freedom from such a fundamental condition affect your thinking/designing of the interior of microgravity or surface environments? Is the human body actually capable of adapting to a fully non-oriented spatial matrix, or do we need, in some essential physiological way, a "plan" to organize our actions in space? Do you establish a datum for action in microgravity?

CA: Yes, we do establish a datum. We call it the "local vertical." It's been established as a fundamental architectural requirement in the U.S. Operating Segment of the ISS thanks to lessons we learned from our experiences on Skylab and Mir. About two-thirds of the Skylab orbital workshop module was just open space with equipment all the way around the outer perimeter. They had water tanks going around the circumference. You have probably seen videos of the crew trying to run around them and they keep falling. What we learned was that in the open part of the orbital workshop, it was very hard for them to function. Every time they would turn around, they would get disoriented, whereas in the small cramped crew living quarters at one end (a part for which industrial designer Raymond Loewy did some designs) there was a clearer sense of up and down. So NASA established the local vertical as a requirement. It's interesting to note that during the same time, the Soviets also established that having a basic vertical datum improved crew productivity, because the last few Salyut stations designed in the mid-1970s had the same basic interior architecture we still see today in the ISS's Russian-built service module. Now, if you go into a module, as long as you don't turn more than 90 degrees in the X and Y planes, those modules have to maintain the same local vertical. But if you're moving in a Z-axis, as in going up or down, you can change local vertical.

(top)
Astronaut James S. Voss
performs a task at a
workstation in the Destiny
laboratory as astronaut Scott
J. Horowitz arrives from the
space shuttle *Discovery*.

(bottom)
Crewmen eating in the
orbital workshop wardroom
of the Skylab 3 space station
in Earth orbit. Astronaut Alan
L. Bean (right) illustrates
eating under zero-gravity
conditions.

KK: How does the local vertical get encoded, physically?

CA: My colleague Rod Jones developed what turned out to be the main rubric for U.S. modules on the ISS, and it's rather elegant: it's mainly about light. We put the lights in the plane that we call the "ceiling," or "overhead," and the air vents and other equipment can go at the opposite end or at the "bottom." Light comes from above, that's the number one thing. Then all the labeling aligns with it. Then there is seat track, like Boeing uses in their planes, on the front of all of the equipment racks for attaching portable grips that you just plug in and tighten down. The crew uses the rail for handrails, foot restraints, for anchoring all kinds of things.

KK: How do such standards get negotiated? Do you think that there are lessons to be learned here about how different interests negotiate the use of space, or do the extremely stringent parameters simply conspire to produce a formally organic whole?

CA: It's *Städtebau.*

KK: *Städtebau?*

CA: My undergraduate degree was in social studies, including economics, government, and sociology. My focus was the phenomenon of the city as an organic whole, as a kind of entity unto itself, a complex of social relations that intensifies as density of inhabitation increases. And the same is true of metabolic exchanges. To me, the city, even though it is created by humans, is a natural phenomenon. We are a part of the planet, and we have developed a rhythm of density and looseness that was pretty well balanced for a long time. When I graduated from Yale School of Architecture, I took a position in Tange's office in Tokyo. I would get off the train a couple of stops early and walk past his Yoyogi gymnasium at night on my way home. It's an incredible building with a metabolic balance between structure, space, and life cycle. After Japan I went to Berlin. I was there for the really good times: the Wall had come down and all hell was breaking loose. In Berlin I learned to love Bruno Taut. He is terribly underrepresented, at least in America. There are parts of *Hufeisensiedlung* that people don't seem to study, such as the *Kleingarten* colony around the outside of the main *Hufeisen*. The relationship between the forced perspective of its little entryways, and the shared and the private green spaces behind the houses actually maximize the sense of space and the communal use of a really small area of land. And these small houses were quite livable because of their relationship to the exterior in these tiny little culs-de-sac. Most people don't even look at those buildings. Most of the work that I did in Germany was urban design for small towns in Brandenburg that needed new master plans. I was doing my best to reproduce Taut's urban ideas. And the ISS is an international community. It's a city with its own metabolism.

KK: If the ISS is like a planned city, is there a supranational entity in charge of the overall interior arrangement of the ISS modules? Is there a master plan, an international zoning regulation?

CA: No. It figures, right, that this project was conceived in Houston, which is a city that has no zoning. There was never a zoning code written for the ISS. The U.S. Operating Segment originally had standardized capabilities for each module to enable reconfiguration as necessary over time, but those got nickeled-and-dimed out of each as they were built. The Russian segment has its own set of near-rules, and the constant effort to keep both systems working together is really extraordinary.

KK: But the geometry exerts a regulating force.

CA: It does. And good old physics exerts a similarly ineluctable set of rules, through the reality of orbital mechanics. The original geometry was intended to enforce a volume that was considered pretty much optimal for people in microgravity. What you have in section is a seven-foot-square open space inscribed in a fourteen-foot diameter circle. Equipment lines all four sides, and the resulting voids in the corners carry utilities. Seven-by-seven feet works well because what we learned in the orbital workshop in Skylab is if you're in the middle of the room, you're stuck. There's no way to get to somewhere that you can hold on to or push off from. Air is very different from water that way!

KK: This configuration gives the Vitruvian figure a completely different meaning. I have a question about windows, or more generally about the relationship of this radical interior to the exterior. The window condenses so many issues relevant to the history of the interior: the framing of view, the construction of landscape, the armature for perspective space, the sentimental frame of longing, not to mention providing light and fresh air. I noticed that all space vehicles seem to have windows. Do any of these functions play a role in space? What do astronauts actually experience through the window?

CA: A great deal of the earth science that we have done that has helped to drive our collective awareness of what's happening to our planet is performed by astronauts simply observing the planet. Whenever they are given free time, the crew will look at the earth. That's what they do. The crew insists on the windows. Daytime is dictated by how many times you've been around the planet, so the circadian rhythm is completely whacked out. There are sixteen sunrises and sixteen sunsets in twenty-four hours for them. By the time they have lunch after they launched, they have gone around the earth four times.

(top)
Embroidered EVA (Extra
Vehicular Activity) suit patch,
worn on the left shoulder
of space shuttle astronauts'
"space" suits.

(bottom)
Astronaut Karen Nyberg looks
through a window in the Kibo
laboratory of the ISS.

KK: You developed an LED light fixture to replace the standard fluorescent bulb in response to this problem, right?

CA: Yes. On ISS, which was originally designed over twenty years ago, we currently use regular fluorescent bulbs that have triple seals around them. So they're huge. They're three times as heavy. They cost a quarter of a million dollars apiece and they burn out a lot. However, with LEDs and a very simple software, you could code fixtures to shift your color temperature from dawn to midday to evening, a red-yellow-blue-pink-purple-spectral shift over twelve hours, so that you have a sense of a day passing, and of what time of day it is.

KK: Earlier you raised a question of style. It is generally assumed that there is the equivalent of an "industrial vernacular" associated with highly technical design projects, and that a project like the ISS interiors would certainly fall outside of any discussion of aesthetics or taste. In fact, a presentation by your colleague Kriss Kennedy is titled "The Vernacular of Space Architecture." The term vernacular has been neatly defined by Yi-Fu Tuan as pertaining to artifacts so subject to given conditions and local restraints that they naturally tend toward the typical, unauthored, fashion-free objects that we call the vernacular. If this definition is transposed to your field, it would be the stringent environmental conditions that would constitute the restraint on your design agency and that produce something like a high-tech vernacular. Can you look at a space vehicle or a space interior or a piece of equipment and identify a style?

CA: I can probably tell you who made it. It has a lot to do with materials, color, and processes. I can tell Russian hardware from American hardware, Japanese hardware from American hardware, even if it's the same blueprint. There's a different standard of craftsmanship. There is a little something different about the user interface, usually the handle, a place that's not absolutely predetermined by function.

And it will have a slightly different shape. It will have a different color. Coming upon Russian equipment, you recognize those colors, the dark reds and the browns and the green, the moss green. The building where I lived on Alexanderplatz, in East Berlin, was all done in those colors. The Russian modules are a little bit more like *Nautilus* than they are like *Discovery*. I'm talking about two important vehicles in science fiction. The *Nautilus* was Captain Nemo's ship, with a fine Victorian sense of luxury. With *Discovery* in *2001: A Space Odyssey*, Stanley Kubrick succeeded in setting a kind of standard of style that is still our highest aspiration. We're not even close to it, of course, in terms of our finished product. It's a rigid, cold, inexpressive, male culture of the blue and the white. All of the worst qualities of the organization man come out in *2001*, and I think that that's still kind of what our program seems to hold as an ideal, unfortunately.

KK: In the late 1960s, Loewy was asked to design the interiors for NASA's Skylab. His project looked remarkably like the plan of Buckminster Fuller's Wichita Dwelling Machine of the mid-1940s.

CA: Loewy did a complete design but this was because Jacqueline Kennedy said "Oh, Raymond just did Air Force One for us, it's fabulous. You must get him." So somebody at JSC said, "Absolutely, Mrs. Kennedy." And they got Loewy to come in.

KK: I saw a design that you did for a lounge in the ISS.

CA: I did a lounge for the Pirs Module. *Popular Science* wanted to do a study turning the ISS into a commercial hotel and the Pirs airlock into a honeymoon suite. It's a really bad choice. Generally, I am against these kind of trivializing schemes, but I suppose there is at least one advantage of using an airlock for a bedroom. Remember, you can't shove your partner out the lock without going out yourself, so you really are in this thing together!

Portfolio: Petra Blaisse

Lois Weinthal

Working with her office, Inside Outside, Petra Blaisse has invented a series of material explorations that challenge the accepted notion of the wall as it traditionally has been imagined in architecture, and represented in architectural drawing. In the practice of architectural drawing, a wall is illustrated as a line. That line denotes an absolute fixed position; it contains no information about material or temporal qualities. While it is a defining moment in architecture's history, the technological and ideological development of the curtain wall merely substituted one absolute for another: the wall is transparent rather than solid. Using both low- and high-tech construction techniques more closely aligned with textiles than architecture—knitting, knotting, shrinking, pleating, and laser-cutting—Blaisse's explorations of the "curtain wall" complicate and question this binary, giving the wall thickness, tactility, and dynamism, differentiating between inside and outside in a way that necessitates an entirely new approach to representation.

Blaisse wraps the interior in textiles, much like clothing wraps the body. She tailors the materials in order to accommodate and mediate the body's sensual responses. For instance, where acoustics need to be dampened, as in the espresso bar of the Mercedes-Benz Museum in Stuttgart, Germany, she heightens the visual quality of patterns and texture. A brushlike wall covering projects into the room to help absorb sound. Visual attention is pulled to the perimeter of the space, inviting the hand to sweep across the wall surface. Both hand and eye are needed to process the soft quality that breaks from conventional wall surfaces.

Once installed, Blaisse's textiles help negotiate the scale of body and architecture. The sensual qualities attained through these materials do not fit within the conventions of architectural representation as two-dimensional surfaces. The standard thick black lines are replaced by flexible lines to illustrate textiles. These lines are not static: they are activated into three-dimensional forms by the environment and user. For example, on the seventh floor of the museum, a curtain provides visual porosity while controlling light that enters from the ceiling above and an open atrium below. A finlike curtain on one side hints at the lacelike pattern on the other. When both sides overlap and are viewed together, the layering and structure of the curtain is revealed, unlike the opacity of a wall that hides structure within its thickness.

In a residential project, a bright fuchsia curtain draws attention to the surrounding terrain, as the concentrated pink confronts the green landscape behind it through a floor-to-ceiling window. In one configuration of the curtain, daylight produces a planetarium-like space in which multiple apertures create the effect of dappled light rays. The curtain turns the interior into a sundial by registering the movement of the rays and the passing of time. The temporal sensitivity of this wall cannot be depicted using conventional drawing. In response Blaisse has invented her own methods of representation.

Her design process often begins with a drawing that highlights the location of curtains and the space-making forms they will take. Color and fluidity are the dominant elements that emerge and take precedence over the architectural shell. Once the interior site has been established, the programmatic requirements are matched to textiles (in turn, these undergo a series of experiments in layering in order to develop a range of translucencies that are often coupled with patterns). In the design of curtains for the Toledo Glass Pavilion in Ohio, Blaisse's textile samples include methods of layering voile, then sewing the layers together with stitch lines that provide a complementary pattern; or silkscreening directly onto white tulle with a white-and-gold dot design. The same silkscreening process translates across textiles and is applied to a heavier blackout curtain to manage light at the perimeter of the building.

Blaisse confronts the conventional idea of the wall and the curtain by starting with the interior experience. For her, the answer is not found in a single material or bolt of fabric; instead, it is the flexibility of textiles and the experimental nature of opening and closing that Blaisse builds upon. Expected effects are tested in samples but the final installation leaves room for unexpected surprises often found in the desire to touch. These curtains accomplish the programmatic function of dividing one space from another, and are also a performance in themselves. The curtains break from traditional uses and provide the equivalent of alternative architectural practices that support new interpretations of interior space making.

Petra Blaisse started her career at the Stedelijk Museum in Amsterdam, in the Department of Applied Arts. From 1987, she worked as a freelance designer and won distinction for her installations of architectural work. Gradually her focus shifted to the use of textiles, light, and finishes in interior space and to the design of gardens and landscapes. In 1991, she founded Inside Outside. The studio works in a multitude of creative areas and across disciplines, including textile, landscape, and exhibition design.

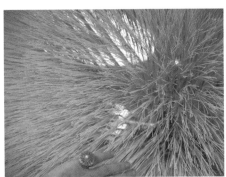

Mercedes-Benz Museum,
Stuttgart, Germany, 2004–6

(top and bottom)
Brush wall for acoustic
regulation in the espresso bar

Lime-green finned curtain with
black backing

Mercedes-Benz Museum,
Stuttgart, Germany, 2004–6

(top and bottom)
Outside the space-creating
darkening curtain on the first
floor, and detail of split and
seam

(opposite)
Inside the space-creating
darkening curtain

 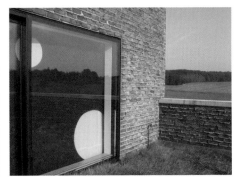

Villa Leefdaal,
Leefdaal, Belgium, 2003—4

(top)
Living room with curtain pulled
closed meeting the glass wall
and landscape

(bottom, left and right)
Villa in the landscape, and view
outside a bedroom with pink
circles

Bedroom with perforated curtain

<u>Toledo Glass Pavilion</u>,
Toledo Museum of Art,
Toledo, Ohio, 2002–5

(top)
Sample curtain of silkscreened
dots and floral pattern on
blackout curtains

(bottom)
Sample curtain of silkscreened
dot pattern on tulle, with white
dots on one side and golden
dots slightly shifted on the other

(top)
Sample of a layered curtain

(bottom)
Drawing showing overview
of curtains

Acknowledgments

Contributors

This publication has been made possible by grants from the Graham Foundation for Advanced Studies in the Fine Arts and Parsons The New School for Design. Special thanks are due to Jamie Drake and Victoria Hagen for their early support of the *After Taste* symposia. The participants in the conferences charged the topic with their intellectual contributions, and we wish to especially acknowledge their collective role in stimulating our thoughts. Susan Senazy, Jonsara Ruth, Alfred Zollinger, Ioanna Theocharopoulou, Johanne Woodcock, Mayer Rus, and Donald Albrecht all offered sharp and critical insights for which we are grateful. Little would have been possible without the administrative support of Christine Chang, Howard Leung, and Alan Bruton, and we would not have images without the assistance of Elvan Cobb and Lee Gibson. At Cornell University, we extend special thanks to Robert Barker, Aaron Goldweber, Beth Kunz, Danielle Mericle, and Lyn Pohl. Finally, we are grateful to Princeton Architectural Press, especially our designer, Jan Haux, and our editors, Jennifer Thompson and Megan Carey, who offered invaluable guidance throughout this project.

Kent Kleinman is the Gale and Ira Drukier Dean of Cornell University's College of Architecture, Art, and Planning. His scholarly focus is twentieth-century European modernism, and his publications include *Villa Müller: A Work of Adolf Loos* (1997); *Mies van der Rohe: The Krefeld Villas* (2005); and a translation of Jan Turnovsky's *The Poetics of a Wall Projection* (2009).

Joanna Merwood-Salisbury is associate professor of architecture at Parsons The New School for Design. Trained as an architect in New Zealand, she received her doctorate from Princeton University in 2003. Her book, *Chicago 1890: The Skyscraper and the Modern City*, was published in 2009. She is currently researching the history of interior design education at Parsons School of Design.

Lois Weinthal is associate professor and graduate advisor for the Master of Interior Design Program in the School of Architecture at the University of Texas at Austin. Previously she was director of the Interior Design Program at Parsons The New School for Design. She is editor of the interior design theory reader, *Toward a New Interior: An Anthology of Interior Design Theory* (2011). She received her master of architecture from Cranbrook Academy of Art and bachelor of architecture from the Rhode Island School of Design.

J. M. Bernstein is University Distinguished Professor of Philosophy at the New School for Social Research. His writings include: *The Fate of Art: Aesthetic Alienation from Kant to Derrida and Adorno* (1992); *Adorno: Disenchantment and Ethics* (2002); edited and introduced, *Classic and Romantic German Aesthetics* (2003); *Against Voluptuous Bodies: Late Modernism and the Meaning of Painting* (2006). He is currently working on a book tentatively titled *Torture and Dignity*.

Alex Kitnick earned his doctorate from the Department of Art and Archaeology at Princeton University in 2010. He edited the volume *Dan Graham* (2011) and has written for the *Journal of the Society of Architectural Historians*, amongst other publications. He has taught at the School of Visual Arts in New York and at Vassar College.

Jorge Otero-Pailos is an architect, artist, and theorist specializing in experimental forms of preservation. He is assistant professor of historic preservation in Columbia University's Graduate School of Architecture, Planning and Preservation. He is the founder and editor of the journal *Future Anterior*, and the author of *Architecture's Historical Turn: Phenomenology and the Rise of the Postmodern* (2010), which traces the intellectual origins of postmodern architectural theory. His installations have been exhibited at the Venice Art Biennial (2009) and the Manifesta European Contemporary Art Biennial (2008).

Julieanna Preston is a director of research and post-graduate studies at the College of Creative Arts, Massey University, Wellington, New Zealand. Her expertise lies in cross-disciplinary creative practice-led research including interior design, architecture, landscape archi-tecture, philosophy, women studies, and fine art. Her research addresses topical themes such as atmosphere, interior theory, wilderness, feminist spatial practice and tooling, and material un-doing and re-doing, generating a philosophy around furnishing and furniture, material surface, ornament, structure and digital technologies, design and politics, design writing, pedagogy for design research, interior detailing and construction, craft, and spatial inhabitation.

Penny Sparke is a pro vice-chancellor and the director of the Modern Interiors Research Centre at Kingston University, London. Between 1972 and 1999 she taught design history at Brighton Polytechnic and the Royal College of Art. She has published over a dozen books focusing, since the mid-1990s, on the relationship between design and gender. Her books include *As Long as It's Pink: The Sexual Politics of Taste* (1995); *Elsie de Wolfe: The Birth of Modern Interior Decoration* (2005); and *The Modern Interior* (2008).

Anthony Vidler, a critic and historian of architecture and urbanism, is dean and professor at the Irwin S. Chanin School of Architecture, The Cooper Union. His most recent books are *James Frazer Stirling: Notes from the Archive* (2010) and *The Scenes of the Street and Other Essays* (2011).

Susan Yelavich is an assistant professor in the School of Art and Design History and Theory at Parsons The New School for Design. Her publications include *The Edge of the Millennium* (1993), *Design for Life* (1997), *Inside Design Now* (2003), *Profile: Pentagram Design* (2004), and *Contemporary World Interiors* (2007). She was awarded a Rome Prize in Design from the American Academy in Rome in 2003–4.

Image Credits

All images credited in caption unless otherwise noted:
21: Courtesy Acanthus Publishing; 22, 25 (top): Penny
Sparke; 23, 25 (bottom): Courtesy of Bobst Library, New
York University; 36–37: Courtesy of the National Library
of Medicine; 58–59, 69: Courtesy the Division of Rare and
Manuscript Collections, Carl A. Kroch Library, Cornell
University; 60: Courtesy the Institut National d'Histoire
de l'Art, Bibliothèque, Collections Jacques Doucet; 64–65:
Courtesy the Anne and Jerome Fisher Fine Arts Library,
University of Pennsylvania; 71: © Serge Stone. Courtesy
the Akademie der Künste, Walter Benjamin Archive; 73:
Courtesy Paterson Marsh Ltd., London; 112: *Interiors* 124
(May 1965): 10; 115 (top and bottom), 117 (top and bot-
tom), 121 (bottom): Parsons School of Design Alumni
Association records, Anna-Maria and Stephen Kellen
Archives, Parsons The New School for Design; 115 (top):
PIC.03.002, box 13, folder 1; 115 (bottom): PIC.03.002,
box 17, folder 14; 121 (bottom): PIC.03.002, box 17,
folder 8; 124–25: *Interiors* 126 (June 1967): 120–25; 132
(top): Courtesy of Plan59.com/Juniper Gallery; 132 (bottom) Courtesy of the Smithson Family Collection; 215:
NASA; 217: S124-E-007975 (9 June 2008). NASA; 219
(top): STS105-304-025 (10–22 August 2001). NASA; 219
(bottom): (1973-08-01). NASA; 223 (top): NASA; 223
(bottom): S124-E-008613 (10 June 2008). NASA